S udying Early Years

Available
Just Ask

Studying Early Years

A Guide to Work-based Learning

Anne Rawlings

 Open University Press

Open University Press
McGraw-Hill Education
McGraw-Hill House
Shoppenhangers Road
Maidenhead
Berkshire
England
SL6 2QL

email: enquiries@openup.co.uk
world wide web: www.openup.co.uk

and Two Penn Plaza, New York, NY 10121–2289, USA

First published 2008

A catalogue record of this book is available from the British Library

ISBN ISBN 13: 978 0 335 21993 3 (PB) 978 0 335 21994 0 (HB)
ISBN ISBN 10: 0 335 21993 4 (PB) 0 335 21994 2 (HB)

Library of Congress Cataloging-in-Publication Data
CIP data applied for

Typeset by YHT Ltd, London
Printed in UK by Bell and Bain Ltd., Glasgow

The McGraw·Hill Companies

Contents

Acknowledgements   vii

Foreword   ix

Introduction   1
Anne Rawlings

PART 1: CHALLENGE   12

1   Early years work-based learning: a modern-day context   15
Anne Rawlings
Questioning your certainties   19
Creative contemporary developments   21
The Key Components Framework for work-based learning   22
References   27

2   Examining the early years field: a practitioner's perspective 29
Daryl Maisey
Working with parents   37
References   38

3   A 'grow model' for work-based learning   41
Helen Sutherland and Jo Dallal
Study skills   41
Learning styles   50
Dimensions   51
Summary   59
References   59

4   Ethics, beliefs, and values in early years   61
Anne Rawlings
Personal philosophies, values, and beliefs   62
Autonomy and respect for children and their views   66
Why we need ethical principles   68
Integrity   71
Policy and pedagogical practice   73
References   74

**5 Working with others: identifying and extending a
    professional and personal baseline**   77
    Anne Rawlings
    The Childcare Act 2006   80
    The Common Assessment Framework   81
    Working within an integrated framework   82
    Observing a concern/issue/conflict/debate   84
    Multi-professional workshop group activity   85
    References   90

PART 2: PRACTICE   91

**6 Contemporary issues in relation to early years theory
    and practice**   93
    Anne Rawlings
    Acknowledging and considering children's culture today   94
    Cultural considerations for a play-based environment   98
    Dispositions   99
    References   103

7 Work-based practitioner: learning to research   106
    Anne Rawlings
    Practitioner research methodology   106
    Question categories   107
    Collecting evidence: what am I going to collect and how am I going
        to collect it?   109
    Types of observations   116
    Research planner/timeline   117
    Key areas for the future   119
    References   120

PART 3: IMPACT   121

8 My learning journey: practitioners' perspectives   123
    Anne Rawlings
    Dolly Walker – my learning journey   124
    Jacky Brewer – my learning journey   125
    Zöe Hale – a talk at the Children's Development Council celebration
        evening   128
    Conclusion   130

    Appendices   131
    Index   141

Acknowledgements

First, I would like to express my deepest gratitude to the people who helped me with the development of this book. It could not have been written without the unstinting support of the dedicated Early Years Team in the Faculty of Arts and Social Sciences, School of Education Kingston University: Daryl Maisey, Helen Sutherland, Christine Lawless, Lalitha Sivalingham, and Liz Tyzack-Jones. Thanks in particular to Jessica Johnson for her insights and contributions to Chapters 4 and 7.

I wish to thank my family for their love, interest, and encouragement. A special thank you to my sister Jane Steward (now retired) who worked with me to build the firm foundations for the degree that have proved to be so successful in the long term. Thanks also to Lyn Trodd, who willingly gave us both information and support in those early writing days to enable us to go forward with confidence.

Members of the Further Education College staff in the Kingston University Consortium have worked with us from the start to build a sound framework for the degree via work-based learning, which has come through several QAA collaborative inspections with many commendations. They are a joy to work with.

The development of the sector-endorsed Foundation Degree in early years has been an amazing development nationally and it can be too easy to forget that, initially, many people had to take risks academically, financially, and experientially to bring the degree to fruition. Eternal gratitude goes to Mary Bousted, Larry Roberts, John Roberts, Molly Pawley, and David Miles for listening and believing that early years workers are worth the risk. The students who were the first cohort through the Foundation Degree all went on to further study and to become role models, mentors, and support for those following in their footsteps. Among them are the first to gain the Early Years Professional Status (EYPS) and some have written about their journeys in Chapter 8.

Andy Hudson, Head of the School of Education, has given heroic support to the early years team when bid after bid arrived. To the students who have as one person put it 'been the pilot princes and princesses of the Early Years Foundation Degree, BA (Hons.) "top up" degree, and the Early Year's Professional Status', we could not have done it without you.

A particular thank you to Alison Holloway, who typed the manuscript and gave me support, sometimes at very short notice. Thanks also to John Steward who helped with his comments and copy reading!

Anne Rawlings

Foreword by Andy Hudson

Preparing those who work with our youngest and most receptive learners to be competent practitioners and reflective professionals is the most important challenge in Education.

These young minds and tiny hands deserve the best that a professional community can provide, yet for many years provision for them, and the many dedicated people who work with them has lagged behind.

It is encouraging to see, at last, the stimulating shift in policy towards the early years sector and rapid change. It is exciting also to be part of a movement bringing the insight of the academy, the gathered observations of our research community and the accumulated 'best practice' of those in the vanguard of early years education together in work based courses.

This volume sets out to gather these elements in an attractive and approachable way, for the student, the policy maker, the parent and the teacher. It draws extensively on our experience at Kingston University's School of Education developing work-based learning for early years practitioners.

It has always been my belief that the University School of Education works best in a thorough on-going partnership with practice, here in this excellent book, are the fruits of that collaboration.

Anne Rawlings sets the scene for an urgent national mission and brings accumulated understandings to our attention in a unique book aimed at those aspiring to professionalise their practice in order to better serve young people.

A commitment to the highest standards in academic work linked to a profound understanding of busy professionals studying and working together underpins Anne's work.

This book is driven by a passion to improve the lives of our youngest and most vulnerable citizens and illustrates a method, derived from experience, of effective university-led work-based learning.

Andy Hudson
Head of the School of Education, Faculty of Arts
and Social Sciences at Kingston University.

Introduction

This book is written to support and challenge early years practitioners who have chosen to study on award-bearing courses in the workplace. It is targeted specifically at those early years practitioners who have reached the National Vocational Qualification (NVQ) Level 3 and above, and who are entering higher education institution courses such as foundation degrees and intend to progress towards a BA (Hons) degree. The book will support those who are studying early years modules within other education courses, such as a degree in early childhood studies. It will also be of interest to students, tutors, mentors, and employers in enabling work-based learning.

The Kingston University Early Years Team developed a work-based sector-endorsed early years foundation degree with its partners. These include further education colleges, employers, early years partnerships, and key members of the surrounding local authorities. It was clear that the demand was there for a new qualification with higher education credits that could provide a career pathway for those experienced early years professionals working in the sector.

Early years practitioners come from a wide variety of settings, including the state, grant-maintained, voluntary, private, and independent sectors. This can present many rich and exciting challenges both for the learner and the institutions running courses. It is important for all to remember that practitioners coming onto such courses arrive with a huge array of life and work experiences. These experiences can be positive or negative, but they all contribute to the 'strength of character' of the individual.

On the positive side, many practitioners are supported by their settings, being given time and a mentor to support their professional development. On the negative side, however, it is the experience of the Kingston University Early Years Team that some practitioners have been told that they 'would not amount to much' or that 'you can do the degree but do not expect me to do anything about it, as I don't need anyone that qualified', and they might earlier in their lives have been told that 'you are not very bright academically and had better go into childcare'. A childcare manager was recently reported in a national newspaper as saying,

> For me, the new early years professional qualification is about raising the profile of childcare. It is often said there are not enough men in childcare, and I think the lack of proper qualifications is one of the

reasons for this. It means that working in early years education is seen as a poor relation to teaching, that those early years are a sort of stopgap before school. Because it is not recognised by the government, it is not recognised by parents either. They have the attitude towards children in childcare of 'well, they'll be going to school to learn soon'.

(Guardian, 3 July 2006)

It has taken many years for nursery nurses, teaching assistants, and early years workers to gain the recognition they deserve and there is still a long way to go. The cohorts across the country currently finishing SureStart sector-endorsed foundation degrees and BA (Hons) degrees are the early years professionals of the future and role models for the new generation of early years workers who are developing personally and professionally through work-based learning. This book is an enabling resource that recognizes early years practitioners do come with practical experience, sometimes over many years.

What is work-based learning?

Work-based learning can take many forms depending on what the learner wants to gain from it. For example, Seagraves *et al.* (1996) suggest the learner may desire specific experience in 'learning for work, at work or from work'. It can be very simple, such as work-shadowing someone to gain a greater insight into a particular role, or complex, such as developing policies and procedures for a new early years unit or children's centre. For most practitioners reading this book it is likely to be a structured learning course, taking place in a paid or voluntary work position that connects career opportunities and interests with academic aspirations and qualifications. This is particularly pertinent to early years practitioners because until recently it has been almost impossible to gain access to higher education qualifications. Most childcare courses are normally gained through NVQ level qualifications and these tend to peter out at NVQ Level 4 and 5. Gaining qualified teacher status, early years professional status or moving on to other multi-disciplinary areas all now require a BA degree and appropriate GCSEs (General Certificates in Education).

The early years sector-endorsed foundation degree (FdA) provides a transition from further to higher education. However, it should also be recognized as a qualification in its own right for those who wish to remain at a senior practitioner. FdAs can be most successful when institutions, employers, and students work collaboratively in making the transition seamless between further and higher education.

The South East England Consortium for Credit Accumulation and Transfer (SEEC 2002) defines work-based learning as 'negotiated, defined and understood by all parties, adequate opportunities and support are provided for learning to occur, and the achievement of the intended outcomes are demonstrated and assessed'. Work-based learners have to cope with the challenges and changes that working in an early years setting present, and many have busy home lives. Managing the home, children, working, and studying can be very rewarding but also stressful if not well organized. Being able to reflect, plan, and think ahead are crucial elements in all work-based learning. Becoming a work-based practitioner learner is also challenging and rewarding but can put learners in a vulnerable position in the workplace. They can often be tired at the end of a working day when attending evening or weekend sessions. It is therefore crucial that access to refreshments, excellent learning resources, and a reasonably comfortable learning environment are available to maximize learning. This book is designed to provide a framework for managing and optimizing different and complex components involved in work-based learning. The text and structure of the chapters will support a framework for the challenges and changes that early years practitioners face on a day-to-day basis, and in recent times there have been many!

It is our experience at Kingston University that mature learners take at least a year to settle into academic studies. Initially, they often need a lot of support with study skills, self-confidence, and a flexible framework to enable them to take 'risks' in their learning and academic writing. If possible, it is worthwhile for mature learners to take a short study-skills course before starting their degree. Some degree courses already provide this service, either as a summer course or through an internet-linked on-line service.

The styles of the chapters are based on a cyclical learning approach, which is often associated with practitioner research. It can facilitate the examination of a wider area or focus at a more specific and personal level. The Key Components Framework for early years work-based study and learning is used as a starting point for identifying needs and to use as a model to support reflection and evaluation throughout the book (see Figure 1.1, Chapter 1).

To enable work-based learning, each chapter will provide starting points to encourage practitioners to begin to appraise their work experience in the light of current theoretical perspectives at a level that asks them to think critically and analytically and to explore and evaluate an idea or concept in more depth. The chapters will demonstrate the cyclical nature of enabling learning and self-belief as a practitioner learner. Another aim of this book is to maximize time for busy work-based learners by guiding them to appropriate areas to access research, theory, and other practitioner practice.

How learners, mentors, and tutors define and develop a shared language and understanding when exploring work-based learning is very important in developing good practice. What does becoming a work-based practitioner learner in the workplace mean? This will depend on definitions in dictionaries, references in books, and how work-based learners perceive their own practice. The *Concise English Dictionary* (2001) states that reflective as an adjective means 'thoughtful'. Practitioner is defined as a person who 'practises a profession' and a researcher is someone who 'conducts a methodical investigation into a subject in order to discover facts, establish a theory or to develop a plan of action based on the facts discovered'. However, in educational academic terms it can mean much more – for example, the learner pauses to think about and organize information gathered from reading, the workplace, discussions, and other activities. According to research by Hatton and Smith, fostering reflective approaches to learning is:

> The capacity to undertake *reflection in action*, which is conceived of as the most demanding type of reflection because it is on one's own practice, calling for the ability to apply, singly or in combination, qualitatively distinctive types of reflection (namely technical, descriptive, dialogic or critical) to a given situation as it is unfolding. In other words, the professional practitioner is able consciously to think about an action as it is taking place, making sense of what is happening and shaping successive steps using multiple viewpoints as appropriate.
>
> (Hatton and Smith 2006: 33–49)

A key aspect of any reflection is the 'thinking through' that goes on before, during, and after an event to attribute an interpretation to the reflection. Thinking through an event, learning point, issue or concern can be supported in a variety of ways depending on the type of learner. For the purpose of this book, the term 'practitioner' will be used throughout, while acknowledging the breadth of work-based experience as well as varied starting points for personal and professional learning necessary to become a reflective practitioner researcher.

There are many problems associated with this type of reflection. For example, a practitioner might find it difficult to be honestly reflective when a piece of work is being assessed by a tutor or that the situation or problem may be too 'controlled by others', as they feel they have no say in the management and leadership of determining ways forward. It is necessary for the practitioner to have access to a range of problem-solving skills and to consciously, rather than unconsciously, use these skills in any given situation. One of these skills is the ability to negotiate with colleagues, mentors, and tutors in understanding the needs and requirements of the course. According to Evans (2002: 17), reflection means 'interpreting one's own interpretations, looking at one's own perspectives from other perspectives, and turning a self critical eye onto one's own authority as interpreter and author'.

Although there are many who question the validity of practitioner research, it is the daily systematic collection of accumulated knowledge and facts over a period of time that can move practice from the ordinary to the extraordinary. However, Haywood Metz and Page (2001: 26–27) argue that:

> everything included under the umbrella of practitioner research should not be called research. They predict that calling for teachers to engage in activities labelled as research on a broad scale may produce as many unanticipated problems as it does benefits.

Over many years' experience of working with practitioners, I have had the privilege of seeing at first hand how well planned and evaluated practice can have an impact on improving provision for children's learning. Some of these practitioners have gone on to present at the British Educational Research Conference, at the Children's Workforce Development Council, and written books about their work. A key aspect of work-based learning is having the ability to take responsibility for one's own learning. This means being able to have confidence and strategies for understanding how the course is designed and organized, and whether the practitioner is a visual, auditory or sensory learner. It also depends on the variety of learning experiences that the practitioner has had before coming on a course. As the early years foundation degree course is primarily for mature learners for whom academic study may have taken place some time previously, a settling-in period, during which they can gain confidence and establish support groups, is key.

Currently, the SureStart (DfES) sector-endorsed foundation degree is written by each validating institution to outcomes published in the Statement of Requirement (SureStart 2000) and the Annex to the Statement of Requirement (SureStart 2001). However, the outcomes may be delivered in many different ways depending on the staff, their expertise, and the institutions' own policies and quality assurance procedures. At the time of writing, the SureStart sector-endorsed foundation degree is about to be re-written in line with the government's early years initiatives, Every Child Matters (2003) and the new Integrated Qualifications Framework (2006). The Children's Workforce Development Council and Department of Innovation, Universities, and Skills have taken over the role of further developing the SureStart sector-endorsed foundation degree. New guidelines are about to be issued in the near future. Until recently, colleges could not validate their own foundation degrees but had to be affiliated to a university. This has now changed and further education colleges can now validate their own foundation degrees. In the future, this may mean that aims, objectives, and outcomes will differ across the country as new degrees are written. Reading through the course outlines, aims, and objectives is thus an essential starting point for the practitioner to ensure knowledge about requirements of the course.

While writing this book, the new Prime Minister, Gordon Brown, has announced the establishment of new departments. Schools are to be run by the Department for Children, Schools, and Families (DCSF) overseen by Ed Balls, and Beverley Hughes will be the Minister for Children and Youth Justice. Dr Mary Bousted (2007: 3) writes, 'including responsibility for welfare in the DCSF recognises the importance of family background for learning'. One of the main goals of Department of Innovation, Universities, and Skills will be to raise graduate skills and oversee work-based learning.

Many universities have strong partnerships with colleges, especially those that have been working to build early years sector-endorsed foundation degrees. A real strength of these partnerships is that the mature students currently studying in the workplace learn to be an integral part of a larger 'learning community'. In visionary settings, this broader perspective can enhance development plans, revitalize and motivate staff, as well as keep everyone abreast of current research, theory, good practice, and policy.

Case studies by the National Centre for Social Research (2006) and the experience of the team at Kingston University demonstrate the impact of collaborative partnerships. For example, the first 38 early years practitioners who gained their BA (Hons) and early years professional status are currently supporting and mentoring others who are following in their footsteps. They are amazing role models of good practice and this bodes well for the future. This network covers a large and expanding learning community where creative 'good practice' can be shared. Some past students provide ideas they would like to share with others in the process of writing this book. Some of their learning journeys are shared in Chapter 8.

After many years of working with early years teachers, practitioners, and initial teacher training students, it is my experience that it is usual for many of them to continue their studies and professional development. However, for many who work in the early years sector this has not been possible due to a lack of work-based opportunities to study at a higher education level. The recent cohort of students at Kingston University who completed their BA (Hons) degree has, without exception, gone on to further study. This is a testament to their commitment to learning and professional development and demonstrates the importance of offering opportunities to those who, for one reason or another, may not have had access to sustained study at a higher level earlier in their lives.

The chapters

Chapter 1 provides a modern-day context for thinking about early years and exploring what that term means. It uses the Key Components Framework for understanding how work-based learning can be explored on a professional as well as personal level. Initially, discussion at an informed level can support developing a common language and understanding as well as providing a platform for sharing good practice and thinking about ethics, values, beliefs, philosophies, and policies in early years settings.

Informal but structured discussions are crucial in providing a platform for problem solving and problem managing, particularly in times of change. Because mature students have skills and experience, they are often more willing to reflect critically and to evaluate in an open forum – although it does take courage and self-belief to be the first! Providing a positive collegial learning environment in which honest and open discussion can take place is essential in enabling the student to become a 'conscious' practitioner.

There are many interlinked and overlapping aspects to becoming a practitioner and each has its own constraints. It is important to know and understand each role so that the practitioner can act accordingly. For example, being a reflective practitioner is partly about being able to recognize in oneself the ability to 'reflect on action' and 'reflect in action' (Schon 1987). In other words, the practitioner is able to make explicit conscious decisions and evaluate resulting actions.

Since 2006, the early years tutor team at Kingston University has collated (with permission from students) 'good practice files' of students' work in a variety of formats depending on the type of assignment they completed. Within the files there are a range of critical reflections that can be divided into five different types adapted from Hatton and Smith's (2006) work on defining reflection:

- statements of facts and experiences;
- descriptive reflections on events and practice;
- critical reflection on events and discussion that may need to be changed, adapted or developed;
- applying learning to any given situation;
- integrating learning from different perspectives to apply to future experience and practice.

To explore personal and professional decision making creatively and then articulate those decisions requires a flexible framework that can be used in any situation, whether it is a challenging behaviour in a child, a management issue or initiating a new teaching and learning approach. Chapter 1 highlights the range of opportunities open to practitioners in affecting change.

In Chapter 2, Daryl Maisey provides starting points for the practitioner to organize and reflect personally on strengths and areas for development in a climate of change. Daryl is an experienced early years practitioner who, in her role as a 'lead professional', has addressed many emerging initiatives. Daryl raises dilemmas in current practice that many practitioners will find they can relate to. She encourages them to reflect on their own experiences within the context of their workplace setting and explore how current frameworks are affecting practice. She discusses with integrity and honesty how the impact of new legislation since the late 1990s has affected practitioners on a daily basis. Daryl talks about how important 'cluster meetings' have become for sharing information and good practice. Discussing and sharing with others how they have managed change, and helped to shape and develop practices in their different settings and networking as part of a larger learning community is vital. The word 'setting' encompasses a wide range of provision from all sections of the community. This chapter encourages the student practitioner to look more globally at the early years field and develop a thorough knowledge and understanding of the local and national context in which they work. Critical issues that arise remain a live debate due to the ever-changing needs in levels of provision. Early years practitioners have always had close links with families and carers; however, these links will become even closer in the future.

In Chapter 3, Jo Dallal and Helen Sutherland explore the interrelation-ships between skills, knowledge, theory, and understanding of work-based practice using the 'Grow Model' to support individual learning. This model provides a framework for thinking about early years and what that means in today's rapidly changing context. Where better to start than with activities that begin to encourage practitioners to value and evaluate their life and work experiences as well as identifying ways forward for individual modes of study. Being a practitioner can be demanding, disappointing, frustrating, and yet exhilarating. This chapter encourages practitioners to organize their learning by using study skills effectively. There are examples of note-taking, reading skills, and time management that address different learning styles.

Ethical considerations, particularly when working with families and young children, can pose difficulties when providing evidence. Chapter 4 exposes some of the ethical problems that exist and sets out structures for discussion.

Sustained practitioner research provides time for ensuring quality and balance in practice. Articulating how current practice is examined over a period of time and evaluated enables others to appreciate, validate, and question findings in a secure atmosphere. It is this type of sustained adult work-based learning and scholarship that is different to short courses, which, in the main, impart information. Reflective thinking is required on many levels, including theory, skills, practice, knowledge of self and others, oral work, and the ability to work with others. The list is endless and takes us back to the Key Components Framework of early years studying in the workplace. As the course progresses, practitioners should gain confidence and the ability to develop and use their own personal and professional frameworks. There are case studies to examine and discuss to help explore any ethical issues that may arise in more depth. The examples are, for some, part of everyday life.

Learning styles may influence how and what information is used in developing an understanding of learning in the workplace. Chapter 4 helps lead the practitioner to continue cycles of learning from theory relating to practice to examine the impact on practice, and build a holistic picture of ways forward for the future. The chapter also provides help in how to ask specific research questions and practise developing target questions that are not too broad – 'small is beautiful' – and also more achievable, especially if the assignment date is not too far away! The important aspects of how to hear the child's voice is included in this chapter.

Chapter 5 seeks to enable familiarity with using the Key Components Framework as a springboard for deeper learning approaches and informed action, as well as enabling reflective thinking. Promoting a learning community is about communicating and sharing ideas, theory, resources, and practice with other practitioners effectively if policy and good practice are to be developed further.

The language used in early years education and care is so important in defining concepts, giving and receiving information, as well as making decisions. In an era when working across disciplines and inter-professionality are the key to safeguarding children, understanding the language of different disciplines is essential. This can be achieved very successfully when courses are being established to incorporate students' training from a range of disciplines. Discussing and describing perceptions and interpretations in a non-threatening and positive atmosphere can sometimes illuminate a mismatch between one's own views and those of another. For example, misunderstandings about curriculum delivery with parents or children can raise issues. Chapter 5 provides structures for working through an issue in a way that takes a problem – real or 'set up' – and tackles it constructively.

Many concerns, issues, and conflicts can arise in the workplace personally, professionally, and philosophically. Learning how to listen and respond to problems constructively whether they are to do with relationships, personalities or conflicting work philosophies is an important aspect of self-knowledge, roles, and responsibilities. Acknowledging triggers to emotions and 'red flags' helps one to respond to difficult personal and or professional concerns. Chapter 5 explores and provides structures to understand and practise conflict resolution skills as essential aspects of learning in the workplace. Working with a mentor is a key area in work-based learning. It can present the student practitioner with a variety of issues to deal with, such as having a mentor who may be younger but has the same qualifications, or who has only had experience of working in Key Stage 1 and 2 and has little knowledge of the Foundation Stage curriculum. Using the flexible discussion steps can be a way of working through how to maximize learning and support with a mentor, which can provide benefits for all.

In the workplace, there is theory relating to practice and there is the reality! Having examined the field using an ethics framework, explored theories, definitions and anomalies, Chapter 6 encourages practitioners to reflect on practice in their current setting. It is not just the setting, theory, and practice that are in the process of development but also the manner in which they are researched. This chapter explores how the practitioner can address issues relating to these requirements and begin to make connections that can be illuminated so as to be improved. Identifying starting points both personally and professionally can be very different for each individual. One early years student can be operating in the workplace from a variety of roles and perspectives, another may be a senior manager, and yet another may be in the early stages of their career. Peer support groups with different experiences collaborating to develop strategies for starting points to investigate and improve practice can be invaluable in developing key questions and exploring issues in more depth. Combining and sharing ideas and resources as a group can be enriching, rewarding, and stimulating.

Chapter 6 provides examples of contemporary issues that are common concerns as starting points for discussion. Students will be able to use frameworks and strategies practised in the previous chapters to ensure focused discussions. Being able to ask focused research questions that refine practice is essential if practice is to be improved.

The work-based practitioner as a researcher attempts, in the first place, to identify where change can take place to improve practice. This is normally through a systematic collection of compelling evidence. Also, the evidence collected should be analysed and critically evaluated. Walsh (2005: 45) argues for a contemporary developmental theory set within the child's cultural context:

'I believe that educators who ignore contemporary developmental theory do not so much at their own risk but that at the risk of the children.' This is a strong statement suggesting that there is an over-emphasis on developmental theory and that the broader implications for teaching and learning today should include wider perspectives such as the cultural context, the local context, the setting itself and the beliefs, values, and expectations of the staff. This will enable staff working with children of all ages to 'begin to see them in all their possibilities and potential'.

Chapter 7 supports practitioners in developing the confidence to learn to 'trust' their own judgements and to look critically and analytically at current theory, research, and practice, which demands a deeper understanding of how research methodology and theory impact on practice. It is one thing to know generally about theorists but quite another to know how, when, and where to apply theory to practice.

Awareness of how theory can emerge from practice depends on a range of skills essential to the student practitioner, including how others are applying and or developing theory. Chapter 7 examines how compelling evidence can come from a variety of sources, including a 'learning log', diary, observations, photographs, tape recordings, children, staff, parents, colleagues, and tests. This is not a definitive list but begins to set out how important it is to set parameters for any area to be 'researched' by the practitioner to evaluate and consider current and future impact.

The final chapter draws together all the components of early years work-based study and encourages practitioners to identify personal needs and goals reached, and to appreciate that their learning, job satisfaction, and career is in their own hands. It highlights the importance of reflection and evaluation in managing change and responding to different situations. Chapter 8 also encourages practitioners to imagine future possibilities as well as celebrate their successes. Practitioners will provide evidence of how their learning has given them confidence to move forward in their development as well as their careers. The contributors to this chapter hope their experiences will support and motivate you to keep going because, as Joseph Campbell (2003) states, 'The rapture of the revelation that *you can do it* is well worth the effort'.

References

Bousted, M. (2007) It takes two to educate, *Guardian*, 3 July, p. 3.

Campbell, J. (2003) *The Hero's Journey*. Novato, CA: New World Library.

Evans, L. (2002) *Reflective Practice in Educational Research*. New York: Continuum.

Hatton, N. and Smith, D. (2006) Reflection in teacher education: towards definition and implementation, *Teacher and Teacher Education*, 11(1): 33–49.

Haywood Metz, M. and Page, R.N. (2002) The uses of practitioner research and status issues in educational research: reply to Gary Anderson, *Educational Researcher*, 31(7): 26–7.

National Centre for Social Research (2006) *Evaluating the Early Years Sector Endorsed Foundation Degree: A Qualitative Study of Students' Views and Experiences*, Research Report #751 (pp. 82–7). London: DfES.

Schon, D.A. (1995) *The Reflective Practitioner: How Professionals Think in Action*. Aldershot: Arena.

Seagraves, L., Osborne, M., Neal, P., Dockrell, R., Hartshorn, C. and Boyd, A. (1996) *Learning in Smaller Companies (LISC)*, Final Report, University of Stirling Educational Policy and Development.

South East England Consortium for Credit Accumulation and Transfer (2002) *Work-related Learning: Precepts and Guidance*. London: SEEC.

SureStart (2000) *Statement of Requirement*. London: DfES.

SureStart (2001) *Statement of Requirement* (Annex). London: DfES.

Walsh, D. J. (2005) Developmental theory and early childhood education: necessary but not sufficient, in N. Yelland (ed.) *Critical Issues in Childhood Education*. Maidenhead: Open University Press.

PART 1
CHALLENGE

1 Early years work-based learning: a modern-day context

Children who grow up with a secure sense of identity and self-worth, who can listen empathetically and express their feelings, learn a 'cooperative assertiveness' that works by establishing a balance rather than learning to dominate.

Sue Bowers

The newly established Children's Workforce Development Council (CWDC 2005) aims to:

> Improve the lives of children and young people. It will do this by ensuring that the people working with children have the best possible training, qualifications, support and advice. It will also help children and young people's organisations and services to work together so that the child is at the centre of all services.

The Children's Plan (2007) sets out its principles as follows:

1. Government does not bring up children – parents do – so government needs to do more to back parents and families.
2. All children have the potential to succeed and should go as far as their talents can take them.
3. Children and young people need to enjoy their childhood as well as grow up prepared for adult life.
4. Services need to be shaped by and responsive to children, young people, and families, not designed around professional boundaries.
5. It is always better to prevent failure rather than tackle a crisis later.

Since the late 1980s there have been many initiatives intended to improve educational outcomes for children (see, for example, Schweinhart *et al*. 1993; National Institute of Child Health and Development 2002). With each initiative and research comes new knowledge and this brings with it new responsibilities. The Effective Provision of Pre-school Education (EPPE) was funded by the Department for Education and Employment (DfEE) in 1996 to investigate three main issues that have important implications for policy and practice:

- the effects on children of different types of pre-school provision;
- the 'structural' (e.g. adult–child ratios) and 'process' characteristics (e.g. interaction styles) of more effective pre-school centres; and
- the interaction between child and family characteristics and the kind of pre-school provision a child experiences.

(DfEE 1997: 2)

The EPPE project accumulated a great deal of important and valuable information about children and their pre-school experiences. The researchers acknowledge the complexity of ascertaining the effectiveness of pre-school provision to track children's developmental progress at ages 5 and 7 years. During the early part of the EPPE project in 1998, several new government initiatives emerged, including the introduction of the Desirable Learning Outcomes for Children's Learning on Entering Compulsory Education (SCAA 1996), Curriculum Guidance for the Foundation Stage (QCA 2000), and the Early Learning Goals (DfEE/QCA 1999). All kinds of research, whether work-based, small-scale or longitudinal, are not without their inherent complexities, if done over a period of time.

Becoming a reflective, 'work-based practitioner learner' can also be fraught with insecurities; the experienced practitioner is being asked to 'question your certainties' (Malaguzzi 1993). As can be seen from the longitudinal EPPE research, any collection of data can be affected or even outcomes changed by outside influences (KCF Strand 1; see Figure 1.2) and frameworks over time. In addition, analysis of data collected in work-based learning on a degree course needs to satisfy tutors that it is appropriate to the specific criteria set and yet demonstrates the practitioner's ability to critique both the process of the small-scale work-based investigation and its out-comes. It is worth exploring the dichotomy the practitioner faces a little further.

In work-based learning where practitioners uses 'real' rather than abstract examples for discussion or small-scale research, they need to proceed with caution. Ethical considerations such as keeping a balance between everyone's needs, including the children, are of paramount importance. How we think and how we act personally and professionally when 'learning and research-ing' in the work setting can have far-reaching effects. It is imperative that a sound infrastructure for researching to learn in the workplace is established early on. Only then can the practitioner proceed with confidence to examine data to improve and or change practice. It is a fine balance between exam-ining one's own practice to improve it and yet ensuring that those around us feel part of any changes. At Kingston University an overriding factor in the current climate of change is that all the people supporting practitioners collaborate at all levels, for example, with local authorities, early years advisory teams, further education colleges, employers, and the practitioners. All parties have an on-going voice in designing and implementing how the work-based learning can take place. All are represented on consultative committees and boards of study that look at how programmes can be developed. Work-based practitioner learning is supported by a team of practitioner network mentors who have already been through the process, as well as other mentors and personal tutors that examine the university's quality assurance procedures. In other words, the practitioner becomes part of a larger learning community. A learning community develops a shared language and understanding, which can facilitate creative ways forward. All members of the learning community are included, particularly the children. This last aspect is followed up in more detail in Chapter 4.

Yelland and Kilderry (2005: 245) argue the case for change by stating that

> Inspired educators confront difficult issues and situations, challenge the *status quo*, and take the lead, following their passion. They act as *agents of change* by re-envisioning early childhood issues and discourses and thereby hope to influence changing practices. They have the potential to move us forward with our thinking via their critical reflections on situations and their viewing of issues from different standpoints without losing their educational commitment.

This is certainly the message that the Children's Workforce Development Council promotes in the new early years professional status. However, affecting change in this way relies on courage, confidence, creativity, sound knowledge and understanding of theory and practice, management skills, and inspirational leadership.

The latest marketing materials used by the Children's Workforce Development Council are about being an 'inspirational leader' so as to be either an effective 'agent for change' or an 'agent of change'. In the first statement, it may be that wanting and agreeing with the need for change it is too difficult to achieve due to particular circumstances, such as not yet being in a defined leadership role. However, in the second statement, the practitioner is in the position to affect change. Recognizing where and how to affect change is a necessary requirement for individuals. This can be implemented in many ways but the inexperienced can be overwhelmed if the infrastructure for work-based learning is not in place.

We are all individuals at a particular moment in time with a particular group of people working in a sector that has, and still is, going through enormous change. Some of these changes are due to the Every Child Matters (2003) agenda and the Children's Plan (2007) with a determined push to work collaboratively across disciplines to safeguard children.

In the workplace, this can present the practitioner with many challenges. Academically, practitioners studying for higher degrees are being asked to examine the theoretical field of multi-agency, multi-professional working to underpin their practice when research evidence to support inter-professional working is in its infancy. Examining theory and research can sometimes be disconcerting, as there are so many seemingly contradictory views on early years theory relating to practice. For example, Canella (2005) suggests that developmental theorists have a powerful controlling influence on the early years field and that 'we are so embedded within our own claims to truth (and their related discourses), that we "forget" that those truths are most likely human constructions, generated within a time and context that supported particular beliefs about the world' (p. 18). It is not the dissonance between different theoretical perspectives that matters but how we respond to the perspectives put before us. How we respond can be as a result of our past experience, cultural background, values, integrity, beliefs, learning, and training.

There is also the continuing debate as to the academic rigour that work-based practitioner research has generated. Is it rigorous enough and is it possible to be both an effective 'restricted' researcher and an 'extended' researcher at the same time? Evans (2002) discusses the difference between being a 'restricted' educational researcher and an 'extended' educational researcher. In brief, the restricted researcher, although regarded as competent, is one who has a 'narrow vision and is generally accepting, rather than critical, of their own practice, which results in their often resisting change and innovation' (p. 11). Evans continues by saying that an extended researcher is one who 'stands out from the crowd' and 'consistently applies a high level of reflection and analysis to all aspects of their work. They seek to extend their research knowledge and skills by keeping abreast of developments in methodology' (p. 11).

This type of extended researcher is often a pioneer who makes a significant contribution towards moving educational research forward. However, Evans suggests that the 'extended' researcher is at the far end of a continuum where books and research papers have been written on the subject of methodology and methodological development and is therefore more likely to be in an educational research community. Where, then, do practitioners fit in that continuum? Are they on a hero's journey? In the workplace, individuals also have their own perspectives, whether it is the child, staff member, parent or carer. It is the combination of learning, researching, and evaluating together that surely pushes and extends boundaries towards an inclusive community.

Questioning your certainties

One of the key ways of opening up a concept is to choose a topic such as diversity and read widely around the subject area, and list all the positives and negatives found when reading. Another imperative is to see, hear, and feel what is happening in and around your setting. According to Rhedding-Jones (2005: 132), 'the seeing and the hearing that happen when studying diversity can be through words, silences, actions and non-actions of adults and children'.

We are all working in an era of change in a particular setting with groups of people, young and old, that gather together on a daily basis. The 'we' of that group are who they are with their own values, beliefs, and identities. You, as an early years practitioner researcher, come together with other practitioners to study, learn, and to gain confidence in challenging current practice so as to make improvements.

Joseph Campbell, a literary scholar, always asked the following question after giving his first lecture to the new intake of students: 'So is it going to be the Grail Quest or is it going to be the Wasteland?' (Campbell 2003: 17). From the question he posed, he challenged the students to keep pushing the boundaries of scientific and creative enquiry to facilitate change. Campbell often reminded his audiences, 'It's not the "agony" of the quest, but the "rapture" of the revelation.'

We all have potential to create and develop something that will matter, to make a difference to a child, family, other colleagues or ourselves. How is this to be made possible? Creative self-development can happen on several levels, but perhaps needs a flexible framework to underpin and provide choices. The Key Components Framework (see Figure 1.2) will provide support, but is not to be used rigidly, and the practitioner can add or ignore any component. It provides starting points from which to develop and can be returned to as an *aide-mémoire*. The components link across and down but all are built on the philosophy that we are able to value each other, communicate effectively by listening well, and have the ability to work collaboratively. It can be used to remind us of the components that affect our learning, practice, knowledge, and understanding when writing an assignment, learning diary/log or just thinking about how to organize necessary reading. Depending on the type of assignment being asked of the practitioner (e.g. presentation, written or verbal), the strands can be used to layer external factors with theory, knowledge of own responses, and impact on practice, just like a 'plait' interleaving throughout an assignment. The Key Components Framework, if linked to the 'Working Ethics' framework in Chapter 7, will ensure that the practitioner identifies what exactly is impacting on their learning for change or improvement.

Sometimes change can be as a result of the cumulative knowledge built up over a period of time through observations and experience, or it can be sudden and unplanned or thrust upon us. What is important is that at a particular moment, stage in a process or significant development, it is recognized by the practitioner and acted upon. In a recent assignment submission by a practitioner, she discussed how she came to a realization during an observational drawing session that too much intervention can possibly hinder a child's self-esteem or motivation.

A practitioner's reflection on respecting a child's view

Children need adults who are sensitive to their individual need to express ideas to enable self-awareness of developing skills, promoting inspiration in other areas. For example, while encouraging the children's line drawings of their favourite animal using the stimulus of 'I Love Animals' (drawings had to include a head, body, legs), they then had to colour their animal. One child coloured his creation of a dog in red – I asked him what colour his animal 'should' be. I then recalled reading 'What is Creativity' (QCA 2000), which guides a practitioner on the valuing of a child's work and guiltily thought of the damage I may have caused to this child's self-esteem. I quickly recovered and asked if this is the colour he wanted and we talked about the colours demonstrated within the book and colours of other dogs we had seen. I realized that I had initially devalued this child's creative expression through stifling his sense of freedom and I began to reflect on how this simple incident could affect him the next time he approaches this type of activity – he may wait to be led rather than attempt for himself or not want to try at all. Self-worth, therefore, is vital to developing the confidence required to take risks which motivate future learning.

For this practitioner, the step was a huge acknowledgement that the child has 'one hundred languages' and that it can be too easy not to listen to the child's inner creativity in an effort to be a 'good' practitioner. I remember well in my first year of teaching the day a child said to me when we were writing some letters, 'Miss, why has the letter "A" got some lines scribbled around it?' It could have been very easy to brush this comment aside in a busy classroom but further investigation showed he had a problem seeing letters as 'stable' on a page. There were two issues here, one was that I was inexperienced and the other that I had been 'tutored' when training to believe that children would always be able to see print on a page and that practice in different multi-sensory situations would be enough in enabling reading and writing. I had to overcome my certainties and take on-board this child's comments and respond to them effectively (Key Components Framework Strand 2). This seemingly small comment led to a lifelong interest in studying how children learn to read and write and I am still learning.

Problem solving in a busy setting or in life situations requires practitioners to have the ability to be creative thinkers. The following philosophy is taken from the old community skills of being able to value others, communicate effectively, and be able to collaborate. Many of these skills have diminished due to changes in modern-day life. Today's children often need to be taught these skills specifically. Many skills are 'hidden' but can be taught and learned. Figure 1.1 illustrates that the problems/concerns are what we see on a day-to-day basis. However, they are often a symptom of what lies beneath the surface. Creativity enables people to break through to new knowledge and learning and this works best when the hidden skills are used effectively.

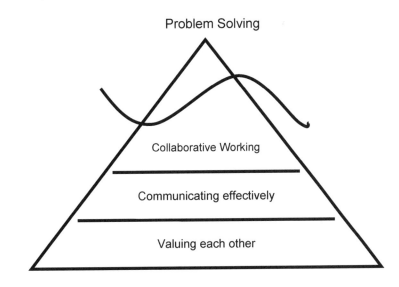

Figure 1.1 Ways and means today (Rawlings 1996).

Creative contemporary developments

Over the past 50 years, creative contemporary developments in education for learning and psychology have done much to promote a more favourable climate for child-centred learning through facilitation. A number of pioneers can be seen to have helped prepare the ground for a teaching and learning approach, which respects the learner's experience and pre-existing skills. At the same time, exciting developments in child psychology and research into how children learn were taking place. (Chapter 3 follows this theme in today's context.)

Jean Piaget (1896–1980) and Bruno Bettelheim (1903–90) demonstrated the profound effects of early learning and parenting on social, emotional, and intellectual development. Carl Rogers (1983) developed a client-centred approach that encouraged further developments in the growth of the counselling movement.

John Heron, of the Human Potential Research Project at Surrey University, contributed greatly to the move away from lecturing and more towards facilitation. New disciplines like transactional analysis, neuro-linguistic programming, the repertory grid technique, and more recently accelerated learning have added to insights and discoveries.

In the commercial and academic fields, Geoffrey Rawlinson (1981) and Edward de Bono (1970) introduced the concepts of brainstorming (now known as mind mapping/showering), creative and lateral thinking. Japanese 'quality circles' illustrated the value of self-assessment. The feminist movement and the growth of assertiveness training, which respected mutual needs, had a significant effect on attitudes and gender awareness. Abraham Maslow's (1943) hierarchy of needs has been widely accepted throughout the commercial and academic world and his later work on what he calls 'peak experiences' has helped to widen our understanding of what has been called the 'paranormal'.

These illustrations represent a tiny part of the explosion of creative energy that has taken place in the last 50 years. Some may question their relevance to life skills or citizenship in schools, learning in the workplace and community. However, most facilitators have seen the profound effect that true affirmation and trust, combined with open, non-judgemental communication, can have on someone to whom these are new experiences.

Many early years practitioners, teachers, and facilitators have noted how a new direction or lifestyle has been discovered and a qualitative change experienced in understanding. It is indeed a holistic approach and many believe it represents a change in human affairs – what Fritjof Capra (1982: 1) has termed a 'paradigm shift' and that 'whatever we call a part is a pattern in an ongoing process.'

The Key Components Framework for work-based learning

The Key Components Framework (KCF) was initially developed for a course I ran for training mediators. It soon became clear that it could be used in an infinite variety of ways: designing a course; talking through how a course is organized; sharing views about a difficult area. The framework is built on the premise that practitioners use their knowledge, understanding, personal, cultural, professional skills and beliefs to underpin work as well as learning. The KFC model has developed over a period of years and student feedback has been invaluable in using it flexibly.

The Key Components Framework can be used to ensure that each strand is used to examine personal and/or professional learning. It is divided into three main strands that interconnect and rest on the 'hidden' skills. It is important to emphasize that the components overlap, interrelate, and complement each other (see Figures 1.2 and 1.3).

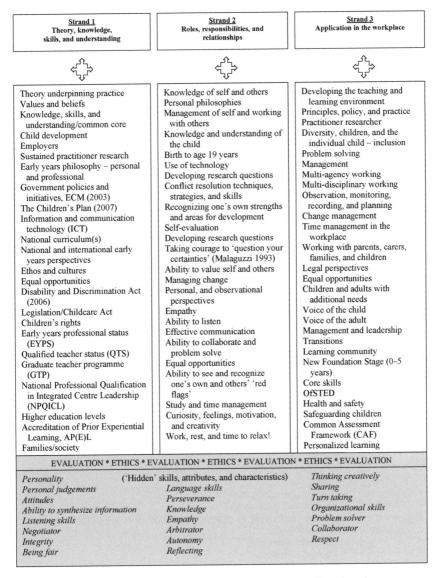

Strand 1 Theory, knowledge, skills, and understanding	Strand 2 Roles, responsibilities, and relationships	Strand 3 Application in the workplace
Theory underpinning practice	Knowledge of self and others	Developing the teaching and
Values and beliefs	Personal philosophies	learning environment
Knowledge, skills, and	Management of self and working	Principles, policy, and practice
understanding/common core	with others	Practitioner researcher
Child development	Knowledge and understanding of	Diversity, children, and the
Employers	the child	individual child – inclusion
Sustained practitioner research	Birth to age 19 years	Problem solving
Early years philosophy – personal	Use of technology	Management
and professional	Developing research questions	Multi-agency working
Government policies and	Conflict resolution techniques,	Multi-disciplinary working
initiatives, ECM (2003)	strategies, and skills	Observation, monitoring,
The Children's Plan (2007)	Recognizing one's own strengths	recording, and planning
Information and communication	and areas for development	Change management
technology (ICT)	Self-evaluation	Time management in the
National curriculum(s)	Developing research questions	workplace
National and international early	Taking courage to 'question your	Working with parents, carers,
years perspectives	certainties' (Malaguzzi 1993)	families, and children
Ethos and cultures	Ability to value self and others	Legal perspectives
Equal opportunities	Managing change	Equal opportunities
Disability and Discrimination Act	Personal, and observational	Children and adults with
(2006)	perspectives	additional needs
Legislation/Childcare Act	Empathy	Voice of the child
Children's rights	Ability to listen	Voice of the adult
Early years professional status	Effective communication	Management and leadership
(EYPS)	Ability to collaborate and	Transitions
Qualified teacher status (QTS)	problem solve	Learning community
Graduate teacher programme	Equal opportunities	New Foundation Stage (0–5
(GTP)	Ability to see and recognize	years)
National Professional Qualification	one's own and others' 'red	Core skills
in Integrated Centre Leadership	flags'	OfSTED
(NPQICL)	Study and time management	Health and safety
Higher education levels	Curiosity, feelings, motivation,	Safeguarding children
Accreditation of Prior Experiential	and creativity	Common Assessment
Learning, AP(E)L	Work, rest, and time to relax!	Framework (CAF)
Families/society		Personalized learning

EVALUATION * ETHICS * EVALUATION * ETHICS * EVALUATION * ETHICS * EVALUATION

	('Hidden' skills, attributes, and characteristics)	
Personality		*Thinking creatively*
Personal judgements	*Language skills*	*Sharing*
Attitudes	*Perseverance*	*Turn taking*
Ability to synthesize information	*Knowledge*	*Organizational skills*
Listening skills	*Empathy*	*Problem solver*
Negotiator	*Arbitrator*	*Collaborator*
Integrity	*Autonomy*	*Respect*
Being fair	*Reflecting*	

Figure 1.2 Key Components Framework (KCF): early years work-based study.

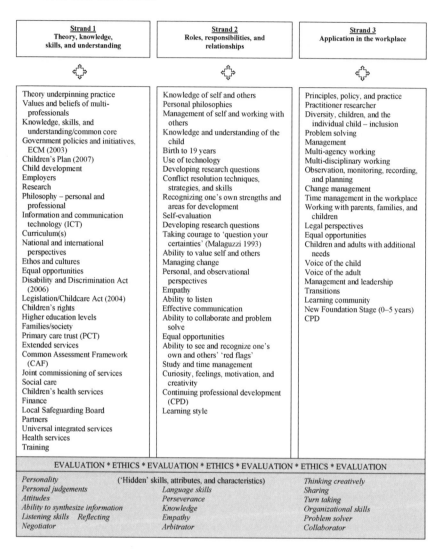

Strand 1 Theory, knowledge, skills, and understanding	Strand 2 Roles, responsibilities, and relationships	Strand 3 Application in the workplace
Theory underpinning practice Values and beliefs of multi-professionals Knowledge, skills, and understanding/common core Government policies and initiatives, ECM (2003) Children's Plan (2007) Child development Employers Research Philosophy – personal and professional Information and communication technology (ICT) Curriculum(s) National and international perspectives Ethos and cultures Equal opportunities Disability and Discrimination Act (2006) Legislation/Childcare Act (2004) Children's rights Higher education levels Families/society Primary care trust (PCT) Extended services Common Assessment Framework (CAF) Joint commissioning of services Social care Children's health services Finance Local Safeguarding Board Partners Universal integrated services Health services Training	Knowledge of self and others Personal philosophies Management of self and working with others Knowledge and understanding of the child Birth to 19 years Use of technology Developing research questions Conflict resolution techniques, strategies, and skills Recognizing one's own strengths and areas for development Self-evaluation Developing research questions Taking courage to 'question your certainties' (Malaguzzi 1993) Ability to value self and others Managing change Personal, and observational perspectives Empathy Ability to listen Effective communication Ability to collaborate and problem solve Equal opportunities Ability to see and recognize one's own and others' 'red flags' Study and time management Curiosity, feelings, motivation, and creativity Continuing professional development (CPD) Learning style	Principles, policy, and practice Practitioner researcher Diversity, children, and the individual child – inclusion Problem solving Management Multi-agency working Multi-disciplinary working Observation, monitoring, recording, and planning Change management Time management in the workplace Working with parents, families, and children Legal perspectives Equal opportunities Children and adults with additional needs Voice of the child Voice of the adult Management and leadership Transitions Learning community New Foundation Stage (0–5 years) CPD

EVALUATION * ETHICS * EVALUATION * ETHICS * EVALUATION * ETHICS * EVALUATION

Personality	*('Hidden' skills, attributes, and characteristics)*	*Thinking creatively*
Personal judgements	*Language skills*	*Sharing*
Attitudes	*Perseverance*	*Turn taking*
Ability to synthesize information	*Knowledge*	*Organizational skills*
Listening skills Reflecting	*Empathy*	*Problem solver*
Negotiator	*Arbitrator*	*Collaborator*

Questions that may be asked about working in multi-disciplinary teams are:

- Who might be willing to actively participate in the transition towards multi-disciplinary working?
- What are the goals and are they realistic and achievable?
- What are the barriers and boundaries?
- Are the collaborative teams able to produce outcomes that are different to those normally achieved independently?
- What are the common interests?
- What are the training needs?

Figure 1.3 Key Components Framework (KCF): Children's Plan (2007).

KCF Strand 1

Strand 1 provides a list that prompts practitioners to consider in what 'era' they are working, to address in more depth their knowledge and understanding in terms of current theory, skills, and research, and to examine how government policies are affecting practice. The items listed are affected in the main by outside forces but impact on how practitioners work in their settings. The language that is used in education and care is so important in defining and conceptualizing early years. A shared language and understanding is key in defining issues and making decisions based on that understanding, and is particularly relevant for inter-professional working. Exploring and discussing terminology within an area, such as years values and beliefs, from different perspectives can illuminate different interpretations, perceptions, and ideals that can support a common understanding.

KCF Strand 2

Strand 2 is about exploring one's own roles and responsibilities within the context of work-based learning. It is also alerts the reader to reflect on how our own actions and feelings affect others. It is very much concerned with relationships because it is the strength of the relationships that can enable a learning environment and make it a creative and satisfying place to work. It does need to be acknowledged that mature learners often have busy lives outside of work, and thus learning needs to be in manageable chunks. This central strand also takes the learner out of a 'comfort zone'. It asks learners to acknowledge and reflect where strengths, areas for development, and emotive triggers are that can support or detract from their learning. This central strand is also about having the courage to take risks in learning, to 'question one's certainties' by examining one's own practice to make changes to improve teaching and learning.

Perception is a process of how we see and understand reality. This is both limited and influenced by our past experience and our present needs. Studying within the context of a work-based course can provide opportunities for challenging assumptions and extending embedded perspectives in a safe environment.

KCF Strand 3

Strand 3 asks practitioners to consider how all the strands integrate in practice. Each workplace setting has its own ethos and culture and depends upon the children, families, and staff that attend the setting. Valuing diversity and acknowledging an ethical framework assures the practitioner that it is possible to improve practice and in turn raise self-confidence.

One excellent way of doing this is to support the exploratory, personal, and professional learning journey. This might be achieved by the practitioners giving a short presentation about the voyage to their current situation. In my experience, many learners are fearful of standing up and giving an oral presentation, particularly about themselves, but it is often a wonderful icebreaker and enables tutors, peers, and mentors to discover things about their colleagues that they would otherwise perhaps never know. It is also a chance for the learner to become reflective and analytical and to realize that they have more abilities than hitherto recognized. This is an exercise that can create a lot of tension but our experience tells us that once

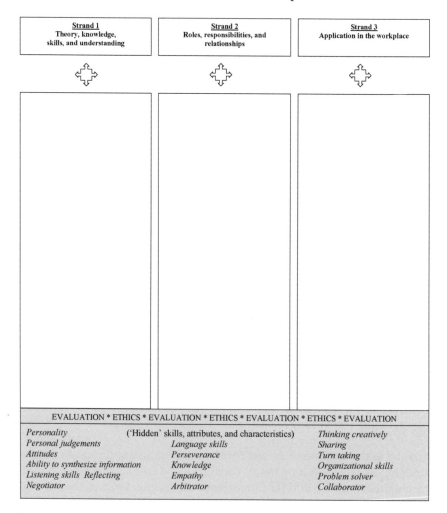

Figure 1.4 Key Components Framework (KCF): Children's Plan (2007) – blank.

embarked upon it can be cathartic and often the first step towards finding inner strength and raised awareness of self-ability. The following is an example of using the Key Components Framework by taking Principle 4 of the Children's Plan (2007) and 'unpacking' some of the issues and current debate around 'services need to be shaped by and responsive to children, young people and families, not designed around professional boundaries'.

Using the blank Key Components Framework (see Figure 1.4), take Principle 3 of the Children's Plan and begin to familiarize yourself with how you can use it to inform and make decisions about external pressures, personal and professional knowledge, and how events, policies, and self-knowledge can impact on learning.

To be successful on returning to study, it is wise to look at the psychology of study to develop good study habits. People exert themselves more when they have a goal to work towards. However, the goal must be realistic so that the learner feels a compulsion to reach it. Hence one needs a clearly defined objective and assessment process. This will link with the four aspects that can be found in the Grow Model (see Chapter 3), which identifies the procedure of creating change or improvement.

References

Campbell, J. (2003) *The Hero's Journey*. Novato, CA: New World Library.

Canella, G.S. (2005) Reconceptualizing the field (of early care and education): if 'Western' child development is a problem, then what can we do?, in N. Yelland (ed.) *Critical Issues in Childhood Education*. Maidenhead: Open University Press.

Capra, F. (1982) Encounter at the edge of the new paradigm (accessed 16 November 2007: www.wie.org/j11/schumcapra.asp).

Children's Workforce Development Council (2005) *Annual Report, 2005–2006*. London: CWDC.

De Bono, E. (1970) *Lateral Thinking*. London: Pelican Books.

Department for Education and Employment (1997) *EPPE Project: Measuring the Impact of Pre-school on Children's Cognitive Progress over the Pre-school Period*. London: Institute of Education.

Department for Education and Employment/Qualifications and Curriculum Authority (1999) *Early Learning Goals*. London: DfEE/QCA.

Evans, L. (2002) *Reflective Practice in Education Research*. London: Continuum.

Malaguzzi, L. (1993) For an education based on relationships, *Young Children*, 47(1): 9–12.

Maslow, A. (1943) A theory of human motivation, *Psychological Review*, 50: 370–96.

National Institute of Child Health and Development (2002) Early child care and children's development prior to school entry: results from the NICDH study of early child care, *American Educational Research Journal*, 39(1): 133–64.

Qualifications and Curriculum Authority (2000) *Curriculum Guidance for the Foundation Stage*. London: QCA.

Rawlings, A. (1996) *Ways and Means Today*. Kingston-upon-Thames: Kingston Friends Workshop Group.

Rawlinson, J.G. (1981) *Creative Thinking and Brainstorming*. London: Gower Publishing.

Rhedding-Jones, J. (2005) Questioning diversity, in N. Yelland (ed.) *Critical Issues in Early Childhood Education*. Maidenhead: Open University Press.

Rogers, C. (1983) *Freedom to Learn for the 80's*. Columbus, OH: Charles Merrill Publishing.

School Curriculum and Assessment Authority (1996) *Desirable Learning Outcomes for Children's Learning on Entering Compulsory Education*. London: SCAA.

Schweinhart, L.J., Barnes, H.V. and Weikart, D.P. (1993) *Significant Benefits: The High Scope Perry Pre-school Study through Age 27*. Monograph of the High Scope Educational Research Foundation #19. Ypsilanti, MI: High Scope Press.

Yelland, N. and Kilderry, A. (2005) Postmodernism, passion and potential for future childhoods, in N. Yelland (ed.) *Critical Issues in Childhood Education*. Maidenhead: Open University Press.

2 Examining the early years field: a practitioner's perspective

Daryl Maisey

If you carry your childhood with you,
you never become older.

Tom Stoppard (1977)

What is 'early years'? There is little doubt among practitioners working with the youngest children as to the importance of effective early educational practice for the acquisition of skills and knowledge required to access learning throughout life. Recognition of the importance for this stage in learning has been a long time coming. Despite pressure from practitioners working with the very youngest children to receive recognition of their professional status, parity in delivering an effective curriculum, and training opportunities consistent with those of their colleagues working in other Key Stages, early years has for too long been seen as the poor relation. Many early years practitioners state that they have been on training courses and been told to 'adapt the materials'. Even the term 'early years' has caused confusion and the debate as to its meaning still rages on.

Ask any educational professional and it can be guaranteed that the term 'early years' will bring forth a variety of responses and definitions as to its meaning as a phase in education. Without doubt there will not be a common understanding. For some, the term 'early years' specifically relates to planned pre-school provision from three years to statutory school age at five years. For others the term refers to the internationally recognized period of early children from birth to eight years of age. Confusion has been further generated by the recent British Government initiative for a new key stage and 'early years curriculum' from birth to five years of age (DfES 2006). Despite discrepancies in the understanding of the term, there is universal recognition that the early experiences of childhood are crucial in acquiring the knowledge and skills required in later life. The research of theorists such as Bruner (1915), Vygotsky (1896–1933), Piaget (1896–1980), and more recently the Effective Provision of

Pre-School Education (EPPE 1999–2006) project demonstrates young children's amazing rate of development and learning during their earliest years, and how important it is to have highly qualified practitioners working with the very young.

Where has early years education come from? The rate of change in early years education has been, and still is, phenomenal. During the early 1990s, teaching and working in reception classes, nurseries, pre-schools, and day care centres was a relatively lonely thing. There was very little guidance and support for staff, and provision and practice was inevitably varied.

There was little or no consistency in effective early years provision between settings and a general feeling of apathy towards early years practitioners from colleagues working with older children. A frequent question from parents at this time when I moved to the nursery after working with seven year olds was, 'When will you be teaching the older age group again, is this a demotion for you?'

The introduction of the National Curriculum, following the passing of the Education Reform Act (DES 1988), began to raise concerns from those working in the field of education, that the curriculum provision for under fives was inappropriate for their developmental needs. There was generally considered to be a 'top-down' push to establish curriculum and assessment procedures in early years, particularly in school-attached reception and nursery classes.

The impact following the revision of the National Curriculum (QCA 1999) and the introduction of the National Literacy Strategy (DfEE 1998) and the National Numeracy Strategy (DfEE 1999) on the curriculum for under fives was particularly significant. In my own experience, and that of a number of colleagues in schools, not only did the staff working with the youngest children have to encompass the new documentation, they also had to absorb the influences that the strategies had on the planning and assessments in nursery and reception classes. Staff in my own school adapted the planning documents in an attempt to aid transition and continuity between nursery, reception, and Year 1. They altered the number and types of assessments to aid monitoring and moderation from the nursery to reception in both numeracy and literacy. Staff felt they were under great pressure to ensure that all the children were prepared and had the necessary skills required for transition into the literacy and numeracy hours (DfEE 1998, 1999) by the spring term of the reception year. It was hard for practitioners to resist the pressure to deliver a more formal approach to teaching and learning in early years.

Despite its flaws, the introduction of the Desirable Learning Outcomes for Children's Learning (SCAA 1996) finally attempted to highlight that children's early experiences were critical to their subsequent development. The document identified that effective early years provision is vital to children's future attainment at school and has a significant impact on the extent to which they are able to take advantage of opportunities later in life. However, the contents of this document were not statutory and many settings that had provision for under fives did not implement the recommendations. The document was in place in some settings for only four years, which was a relatively short period in which to implement, evaluate, and measure any significant impact in support of a separate curriculum for early years.

However, the need for a more holistic curriculum for young children was widely recognized and the Desirable Outcomes document (SCAA 1996) was replaced by the Curriculum Guidance for the Foundation Stage (DfES/QCA 2000). This document identified the importance of a play-based curriculum for children from three years of age to the end of reception year in schools and actively encouraged the involvement of parents. There was a general consensus among practitioners working with young children that the guidance was a step forward in raising the status of early years education and positively influencing early years practice.

The possible advantages of having this holistic framework were endless in terms of support between settings, continuity, and progression. However, the introduction of the curriculum was far from flawless. Initially, only one hard copy of the document was available for each setting with provision for children from three to five years of age. The training for staff was spasmodic and open to different interpretation between authorities. For example, in one authority the training was delivered to a maximum of two practitioners per setting in one day, in a two-month 'window' over June and July 2000. As the document was recommended for implementation from September 2000, it left little time to engage all staff in changes to planning, delivery, and assessment procedures before the start of the new academic year. Compared with the time-scale for the introduction and training for the implementation of the National Literacy Strategy (DfES 1998), which was delivered over a considerable length of time, to all staff, with extensive support materials, there was understandably some anxiety among early years practitioners. This combined with the presence of the National Literacy Strategy and National Numeracy Strategy statements within the Curriculum Guidance for the Foundation Stage (DfES/QCA 2000) caused concern as to the interpretation of a suitable curriculum and resulted in some settings and schools adopting a more formal approach to educating their three- and four-year-olds rather than the play-based curriculum underpinning the recommendations.

For many early years practitioners, it was intriguing that the education of three- and four-year-olds was seen as a separate entity to those younger and older. Despite the Department for Education and Skills (DfES) and local authorities investing in this phase of education and recognizing the benefits of providing young children with high-quality early learning experiences, the misunderstandings as to how young children learn most effectively were still causing difficulties and raising important issues. There was – and to some extent there still is – a common misconception that the National Curriculum should be implemented immediately a child passes his or her fifth birthday while in their reception year. Initially, when the National Curriculum was introduced the general agreement was that the more formal curriculum should not be applied until a child began Year 1, the academic year in which they became six.

The issues and dilemmas facing practitioners working within the Foundation Stage were largely and somewhat surprisingly exacerbated by the introduction of the Curriculum Guidance for the Foundation Stage (DfES/QCA 2000) and raised several further difficulties with transition between, before and after age phases. The differences between the curriculum in the Foundation Stage and Key Stage 1, from a play-based to a more formal approach, was further emphasized and still remains a topic of debate.

What is undeniable and commonly understood among early years practitioners is that the most effective way children learn does not change overnight when they reach five years of age. In reality, every child is different and learns at a different rate and children are not prepared for a more formal style of teaching and learning at precisely the same time. Early years practitioners are acutely aware of the need to know and understand the ways in which young children learn from birth and to where their learning will progress. This is particularly pertinent in light of diversity and inclusion. Early years practitioners frequently work with children and families who demonstrate a vast range of ability and who require different levels of support. There will be children of four years of age who are especially talented and working to targets in level one of the National Curriculum. There might equally be a four-year-old in the same setting who suffers from global delay and requires more intensive support to access the Foundation Stage curriculum. Effective early years practice meets the needs of all children and aims to enable each child to reach his or her full potential through a flexible, holistic programme of teaching and learning.

The aim of the Curriculum Guidance for the Foundation Stage (DfES/QCA 2000) was to establish a common framework for the education of children from three to five years of age, enabling young children to acquire those key skills, such as speaking, listening, cooperation, and independence, that makes for effective learning. It advocated a curriculum through which children could learn through play with enjoyment and challenge. The document included principles of effective early years education and divided the curriculum into six areas of learning:

1. Personal, social, and emotional development
2. Communication, language, and literacy
3. Mathematical development

4. Knowledge and understanding of the world
5. Physical development
6. Creative development

Within each of the six areas of learning, 'stepping stones' indicated progress towards 'early learning goals' achievable by most children by the end of the reception year. The curriculum guidance emphasized the view that young children need to experience a wide variety of opportunities for learning to fulfil their potential. It noted that while all children learn rapidly in their early years, their development occurs at different rates and at different times. The Curriculum Guidance for the Foundation Stage (DfES/QCA 2000) allowed for adjustments to be made in terms of planning, identifying opportunities for assessment and in delivery. In other words, it recognized that all children are unique and it accommodated diversity by enabling individual needs to be met by the delivery of a flexible curriculum.

Soon the guidance was followed by the introduction of the National Foundation Stage Profile (DfES 2002a). This assessment tool further enhanced and supported the holistic development of children between the ages of three and five years. The document encouraged the collection of data about individual children through careful observation, anecdotal and hard evidence of progress over time. It actively encouraged formative assessment and the involvement of parents in collating a holistic picture of the developing child. At the end of the Foundation Stage, the collected profile data informed a summative result publishable to education authorities and parents. It allowed for comparisons between like providers and was seen as a vehicle for the identification of further development and training requirements for practitioners.

At the same time, the Foundation Stage became statutory and was established as an integral, yet distinct phase of the National Curriculum. With the development of the Foundation Stage and the early learning goals, it became apparent that the transition between early education and the greater formality of school was increasingly becoming a complex issue. Surestart (DfES, 2002c) identified the need to work with head teachers to develop the full potential of the Foundation Stage. They recognized the need to build strong and clear links with education in Key Stage 1 and to ensure the development of more provision to see children through the whole Foundation Stage in one place, improving continuity in transition and enhancing parental choice. The aim was to encourage contact between primary schools and the early years sector, improve records of transfer, and encourage 'clusters' of early years providers to link to schools.

Using a common curriculum and assessment framework encouraged local settings, private, voluntary, and maintained, to establish links to share good practice and provide support to each other. Education authorities actively promoted participation in shared training opportunities and, as a result, local providers formed positive relationships across varied and diverse settings. Some areas formed 'cluster groups' or 'early years network groups', which enabled access to lead professionals in early years education and children's services. I was fortunate to be part of this initiative as a lead early years teacher and distinctly remember the excited feeling among colleagues that the early years sector had finally begun to take steps towards becoming a unified voice and a distinct phase in education. The experiences, ideas, resources, and needs of individual settings had begun to be supported and the seeds of a more cohesive and effective early years provision planted:

> This important investment in the early years of a child's education is vital to our ambition of enabling every child to develop their potential. By extending services, promoting greater integration of early years services and enhancing the quality of services, children will begin their primary education better equipped than ever before.
>
> (DfES 2002c)

Following the establishment of the statutory Curriculum Guidance for the Foundation Stage (DfES/QCA 2000), there was a continued feeling of unrest among early years practitioners, particularly in light of the drive for inclusion, that the provision and support being offered for children aged between three and five years was not reflected in the education and care of the youngest children. The publication of *Birth to Three Matters: A Framework to Support Children in Their Earliest Years* (DfES 2002b) acknowledged the importance of learning that takes place *before* three years of age and was a generally welcomed move towards recognition for early years as a unified phase of education.

> It is primarily aimed at practitioners, *Birth to Three* provides information on child development, effective practice, examples of play activities to promote play and learning, guidance on planning and resourcing and meeting diverse needs. The framework also reflects the diversity of types of organised provision for children in this age group and recognises the importance of wider issues including equal opportunities and relationships with parents.
>
> (DfES 2002b)

The introduction of *Every Child Matters: Change for Children* (DfES 2003) further enhanced the need for change in the way young children were educated and cared for from birth to age nineteen. The document was produced in response to Lord Laming's Report (2003) into the death of Victoria

Climbié, a young child who was horrifically abused and eventually killed by her aunt and the man with whom they lived, despite Victoria coming into contact with several different professionals throughout her tragically short life. The *Every Child Matters* document stated that children should be placed at the centre of all policies and procedures involving their education and care. It recommended that all organizations involved in the provision of services to children should work in a more integrated and effective way towards better outcomes under the following five headings:

1. Be healthy
2. Stay safe
3. Enjoy and achieve through learning
4. Make a positive contribution to society
5. Achieve economic wellbeing

(DfES 2003)

Alongside the publication of *Every Child Matters: The Next Steps* (DfES 2004a), the government passed the Children Act (DfES 2004b), which provided the legislative framework for the development of services focused around the needs of children, young people, and their families. The Children Act (DfES 2004b) established the role of the Children's Commissioner and established a duty on local authorities to promote cooperation between agencies and professionals working with children, young people, and their families to meet the five outcomes listed above. The 'Every Child Matters' agenda promoted the notion of the child as being the central pivot of education, health, and social services. It further reinforced the need for a shift in attitude to seeing the development of a child as holistic rather than the child's health, wellbeing, and education as separate entities. The 'Every Child Matters' agenda was generally embraced by early years practitioners and it would appear that a 'bottom-up' push for change was now imminent.

The launch of the new Early Years Foundation Stage (DCSF 2007) also promoted the vision of 'joined-up' thinking and 'seamless transitions' for effective practice in early years by bringing together the 'Birth to Three Matters' (DfES 2002b), The Curriculum Guidance for the Foundation Stage (DfES 2000), and some aspects of the National Care Standards for Childcare Agencies (Scottish Executive 2003). Supporting publications have since further strengthened the shift in provision for early years to become a more holistic, multi-agency, multi-professional way of working with young children.

What is multi-agency, multi-professional working? Multi-agency is generally recognized as a way of working that requires different services, agencies, professionals, and others to work together to provide services that fully meet the needs of children and their families. For this to be effective, it requires the collaboration of information and expertise in a mutually respectful environment to establish early identification of the needs and services required to improve outcomes for children.

For multi-agency working to be successful, it is widely recognized that professionals working in all sectors, including education, health, and social services, need to develop strategic plans to address changing roles and responsibilities. *Every Child Matters: Change for Children* (DfES 2003) identified the need for practitioners to be aware of their own role and to respect the expertise of others for the outcomes to be successfully adhered to, with effective communication and teamwork seen as crucial.

The implementation of the outcomes framework for multi-agency working has appeared to be a move towards cohesion in services provided to children and their families. In the past it may have been commonplace for a child or family, who had been identified as 'in need', to visit several professionals retelling the same story over and over again. Following sometimes numerous time-consuming and costly assessments, they may have finally received the professional support appropriate to the child's or family's needs. On occasion, this may well have involved the child or family working with a number of professionals across health, social, and educational services, each giving input at different locations and at different times. The introduction of the outcomes framework has attempted to address this far from effective form of ascertaining specific needs in early years to improve the provision for all children and their families.

The government demonstrated its commitment to supporting the development of multi-agency working in the early years sector through its Surestart programmes (DfES 2000c), including the provision of opportunities for adult learning and support for parents to improve the drive to eradicate child poverty and to improve access to primary health care and specialist services. The development of integrated children's centres across England has seen rapid development in the way existing services manage their provision. Through the Early Excellence Centre programme, SureStart, neighbourhood nursery centres, and other programmes, the government has intended to create new full-time places where childcare is available to cover a normal or extended day for children from birth to five.

> Many of these will bring together services for families and children through combined nursery education, childcare and family support. The Government is committed to joining up funding streams as far as possible for childcare, nursery education and other programmes targeted on families and disadvantaged areas so that services are integrated and bureaucracy for providers is reduced.
>
> (DfES 2002c)

The strategic vision of effective multi-agency working is to bring about benefits that could not be achieved by one agency working in isolation (DfES 2003). However, it would be unrealistic to expect the transition from existing practice to the successful implementation of multi-professional working to be a seamless process. The introduction of collaborative working with individuals from different professional backgrounds requires considerable managerial skills. Each professional has expertise, experiences, knowledge, and skills that have been directly influenced by their own education, background, and personal attributes. Each professional body has its own methods, practices, and cultures embedded in tradition and history. Partnerships between agencies and professionals need to be developed in mutual trust and respect for multi-agency working to be successful.

There are already moves to address issues arising from the shift towards collaborative working. One of the success factors proposed by *Every Child Matters* (DfES 2003) is the opportunity for practitioners from different professions to experience training alongside each other to appreciate the variety of contributions that individuals can make towards a common goal. The identification of roles of responsibility and clarity of procedures is generally seen as crucial for multi-agency working to be effective. Involving other professionals and understanding different working perspectives are essential to identify the most effective or suitable outcome for individuals and their families.

There is currently the recommendation that once it is established that a child or their family requires support, a 'lead professional' is identified to coordinate the services that may be necessary to address the child's or the family's needs. As these needs may arise at different times and require a range and intensity of support throughout a child's life, the lead professional may change accordingly. The identification of a lead professional appears to be dependent on the true needs of the child or family and may well be employed in education, social services or health. The role is seen as pivotal, acting as a single point of contact for everyone involved, including parents and children. It is anticipated that the lead professional's role will monitor the implementation of any intervention and will coordinate reviews of provision.

Working with parents

There is little doubt that parents are the most influential beings in a child's life. The common agreement that parents are their children's most enduring educators has been referred to in numerous publications and research. From birth it is universally recognized that children develop rapidly, acquiring skills that will impact on their capacity to learn in later life. The involvement of parents during the crucial early stages of development is undoubtedly highly influential.

The success of *Every Child Matters: Change for Children* (DfES 2003) is dependent upon parents being acknowledged as partners working with professionals from different agencies for the benefit of their children. Experienced early years professionals are well aware of the importance of building mutually respectful relationships with parents. Parents know their children intimately and it is essential that their expertise and involvement is encouraged throughout a child's early development.

Until recently, services available to parents and young children have been distinctly separate. Professionals working in health, education, and social services have rarely had the opportunity to liaise together with parents. The shift is now towards providing that opportunity, enabling parents access to integrated services rather than separate professional structures. To maximize each child's potential in the early years, parents are actively encouraged to seek practical support from a range of services available to them and their children from adult literacy, numeracy, and information and communication technology skills through to learning to give practical advice on helping children to learn though play. SureStart (DfES 2002c) supports numerous programmes including 'enhanced childcare, play and early learning opportunities and better access to health services, from ante-natal and baby clinics to specialist services for children with Special Educational Needs (SEN)' (DfES 2002c).

Parents' perceptions, impressions, and relationships with professionals are formed in the early years of a child's life. For many parents, apart from the occasional visit to a health professional, their first and enduring partnership may well start with an early years practitioner and this aspect of the role is not to be underestimated. The initial experiences of working with professionals in early years settings can form the basis for long-term partnerships between home settings and services. As a practitioner, it is essential that appropriate contact and time is invested in forming strong relationships with parents. For effective practice, it is vital that parents and practitioners work together in a mutually respectful environment beginning in the Foundation Stage from birth.

References

Department for Children, Schools and Families (2007) *Early Years Foundation Stage*. London: DCSF.

Department of Education and Science (1988) *The Education Reform Act*. London: DES.

Department for Education and Employment (1998) *The National Literacy Strategy*. London: DfEE.

Department for Education and Employment (1999) *The National Numeracy Strategy*. London: DfEE.

Department for Education and Skills (2002a) *National Foundation Stage Profile*. London: DfES Publications.

Department for Education and Skills (2002b) *Birth to Three Matters: A Framework to Support Children in their Earliest Years*. London: DfES.

Department for Education and Skills (2002c) *SureStart*. London: DfES.

Department for Education and Skills (2003) *Every Child Matters: Change for Children*. London: DfES.

Department for Education and Skills (2004a) *Every Child Matters: The Next Steps*. London: DfES.

Department for Education and Skills (2004b) *The Children Act*. London: DfES.

Department for Education and Skills (2005) *The Common Core of Skills and Knowledge for the Children's Workforce*. London: DfES.

Department for Education and Skills (2006) *Early Years Foundation Stage*. London: DfES.

Department for Education and Skills/Qualifications and Curriculum Authority (2000) *Curriculum Guidance for the Foundation Stage*. London: DfES/QCA.

Laming Report (2003) *The Victoria Climbié Inquiry, Report on an Inquiry*. London: HMSO.

Qualifications and Curriculum Authority (1999) *The National Curriculum*. London: QCA.

School Curriculum and Assessment Authority (1996) *Desirable Learning Outcomes for Children's Learning*. London: SCAA.

Scottish Executive (2003) *National Care Standards for Childcare Agencies*. Edinburgh: The Scottish Executive.

3 A 'grow model' for work-based learning

Helen Sutherland and Jo Dallal

New frameworks are like climbing a mountain – the larger view encompasses rather than rejects the more restricted view.

Albert Einstein

The Key Components Framework will link with the four aspects of the grow model, which identifies the procedure of creating change or improvement (Figure 3.1). The learner will need to identify goals. What needs to be accomplished in the short and long term? At this stage, a reality check is needed. The identified goals need to be achievable, but how are these to be met and when will the process start? Setting bite-sized targets so as not to be overwhelmed by the enormity of the task is an important part of the learning process. An individual learning plan is often a useful tool in helping to identify targets. This approach involves recognizing the barriers to learning and how they can be overcome.

'Procrastination is the thief of time', this is a common human characteristic. The world is full of distractions. The first page is always a huge challenge. Organization is the key to success and an absolute must. Sometimes competition is a motivator and often groups of learners vie for the top marks and the tutor's praise. For others this is dismal, as colleagues always seem to do better. The trick is to start with credible, achievable goals. Interest and curiosity are strong motivators.

Certain modules or assignments spark the imagination and can lead to a deep and lifelong learning interest. It is often a problem that can lead the learner further and further down a learning path and suddenly you can find that you are 'the expert' and others come to you for advice. It is this sustained and detailed enquiry that can be the most rewarding. Each area of study or assignment needs documenting in a 'traceable' way. One of the criticisms of this type of reflective learning is that it is difficult for others to repeat to

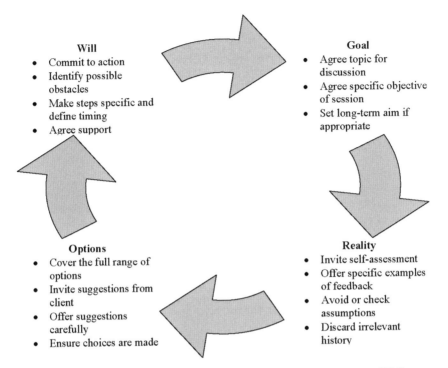

Will
- Commit to action
- Identify possible obstacles
- Make steps specific and define timing
- Agree support

Goal
- Agree topic for discussion
- Agree specific objective of session
- Set long-term aim if appropriate

Options
- Cover the full range of options
- Invite suggestions from client
- Offer suggestions carefully
- Ensure choices are made

Reality
- Invite self-assessment
- Offer specific examples of feedback
- Avoid or check assumptions
- Discard irrelevant history

Figure 3.1 The grow model (reproduced from Quality Improvement Agency 2006).

compare outcomes. However, it is also true that each situation has its own unique set of variables. When observing the work setting, one group of children and staff can vary greatly from another group even in a similar location.

Study skills

Study skills are made up of many facets of learning, including those addressed below.

Academic writing

Academic writing is a combination of the following:

a) *Knowledge and experience.* This is about collecting and presenting evidence to demonstrate the knowledge and understanding you have about the subject area and how this experience impacts on current practice.

b) *Purpose and motivation.* Through the experience of writing con-solidation of learning can take place.

c) *Skill – English/technique.* This is a skill that often needs to be built upon on one's return to study. Issues such as grammar, spelling, structure, paragraphing, and correct referencing all require close attention and to be accurate. A fun way of exploring this information is via Lynne Truss' (2003) book, *Eats, Shoots and Leaves: The Zero Tolerance Approach to Punctuation.* The following quote highlights the importance of correct punctuation:

> A woman, without her man, is nothing.
> A woman: without her, man is nothing.

(Truss 2003: 9)

d) *Application.* A way of applying all of the above to produce a cohesive and concise piece of work so demonstrating academic rigour.

Academic writing: Activity 1

Put the following statements in the order you would use them when planning and writing an academic piece of work.

Keeping to the point
Understanding what the essay title is about
Good English spelling
Dealing with tutors
Deciding where to look for likely sources of information
Re-drafting first draft
Making notes
Discuss with tutor
Sorting out what is most relevant to the topic
Planning
Getting started on the actual writing
Discuss title with other students
Dealing with tutors' comments and criticisms

Taken from an unpublished lecture by Connie Wall (1995)

There are four main stages to the process of academic writing:

a) *Pre-writing.* The first hurdle is to make sure that the question is under-stood. Ascertain what is known and what needs to be investigated.

b) *Planning.* Essential notes need to be made. These then need to be organized and précised to help provide a structure for an academic outcome.

c) *Drafting*. This is when the essay begins to take shape, developing views and opinions, etc. Of primary importance is the introduction and conclusion. The introduction needs to demonstrate the intentions of the work and how they will be achieved. The conclusion is an evaluative summary of what has been written; links need to be made to the introduction and the aims stated here.

d) *Editing*. This is the final stage, which is checked by proof-reading the spelling and sentence construction. It is often useful to involve a critical friend to help with this undertaking.

The following are some questions that can be explored when structuring and writing an assignment:

- What is the purpose of the assignment?
- What must the assignment include?
- What aspects of the subject/area do you know already?
- What additional information do you need?
- Where will you find this information?
- How detailed should you be in developing your supporting ideas?
- What is appropriate – interesting – important?
- How can you organize your assignment effectively?
- Who is going to read it/assess it?
- How can you best convey your ideas to the reader?
- How should you introduce and conclude your assignment?
- References and quoting within the text.
- Bibliography.

Taken from an unpublished lecture by Connie Wall (1995)

A template for a 2500-word assignment might be as follows:

Introduction:	200–500 words
Main body:	1500–2000 words
Conclusion:	200–500 words

Note taking

There are many different ways of taking notes and we all have our own personal style that suits us. Effective note taking is a skill that must be acquired if the workload is to be managed satisfactorily. Study, revision, and written assignments are helped by proficient notes taking and play an important part in the learning process. Whether it is taking notes from books or lectures, these skills need to be developed. Within 24 hours it is possible that most students have forgotten 75 per cent of the lesson, so going over notes plays an important part in remembering what has been taught.

Note taking: Activity 2

Lecturers often structure lessons so that they aid note taking. Handouts are given and main points are often written on the board or provided in the form of a power point presentation. This aids the note-taking process.

- Practice taking notes as the speaker is giving information on the subject.
- Choose a television documentary programme that is enjoyable and informative. This will provide a basis for note taking.
- Record and watch the programme and take relevant notes about the subject for 10 minutes.
- Watch the recording to check that the relevant information has been recorded in the notes.

Answer the following questions:

- What has been achieved by taking these notes?
- Has the relevant information been captured?
- What future uses might these notes have?
- Where will the notes be kept?
- Was increased understanding gained by taking notes?

Developing a personal style of note taking is important as it facilitates the retention of information. Different ways of taking notes include:

- Pattern notes (mind mapping)
- Lists
- Linear notes
- Colour coding
- Numbered points
- Bullet points

For more information on note-taking skills, refer to Stella Cottrell's *The Study Skills Handbook* (2003: Chapter 6).

Example of a section of an early years lecture

Planning should enable the principles of education to be translated into effective practice. Planning is a key factor in effectively implementing the curriculum. It takes into account the learning needs of children within the framework of the curriculum and provides for this delivery to the group. The starting point in children's education is what they know and can do. To plan you need to observe the stage the child has reached, following a continuous cycle of progression and revision. The cycle shows you how you need to be aware of children's individual needs and their understanding.

An example of the use of linear notes is as follows:

1   *Planning*
1.1 Enable principle of ed. > effective practice
1.2 Key factor in implementing cur.
1.3 Learning needs of ch'n within framework of cur. > provides for delivery
1.4 Starting point in ch'n's ed. > what they know + can do
1.5 Plan need to > observe > follow cycle of progression + revision
1.6 Cycle shows need to be aware of ch'n's indiv. needs and understanding.

(*Key for abbreviations*: ed. = education, cur. = curriculum, ch'n = children, indiv. = individual)

An example of the use of patterned notes is given in Figure 3.2.

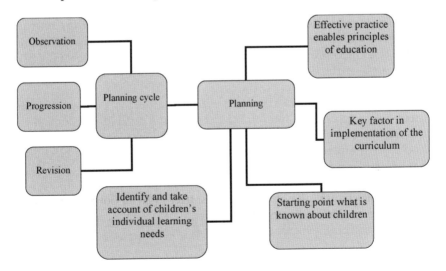

Figure 3.2 An example of the use of patterned notes.

An example of the use of bullet points

Planning

- Effective practice enables principles of education
- Key factor in implementation of the curriculum
- Starting point what is known about children
- Identify and take account of learning needs of children
- Planning cycle
  - Observation
  - Progression
  - Revision

Reading skills

Let us take some time to think about reading and how to do it more effi-
ciently. Most of us do it and the learner would not have achieved a Level 3
qualification without research and acquisition of more underpinning
knowledge. Reading speed can be increased by simple means.

When we read, our eyes do not follow the words in a straight line. An
easy way to make sure that they do is to put your finger or a pencil under the
line and follow it. This focuses the eye and speeds up the reading process.

When there are volumes of books to read, the reader needs to be selective:
look at the title of the book and ascertain whether it is what you are looking
for. Read the summary at the back of the book or at the end of chapters to
determine its relevance. Look at the contents page and select the relevant
chapters. Scan the books or internet sites to find definite pieces of information. It is not necessary to read every word, but a quick glance down the page
should achieve the aim. Look up items in the index or keywords on the
internet.

Remember the skill of skimming, which is a form of selective reading.
Select certain bits of a chapter to read. It is often a good idea to look at the
introduction of a chapter or look at headings, diagrams or tables. It is often
quicker to interpret visual information such as graphs and make brief notes
that are saved and used as information for an assignment.

When reading/researching for an assignment, it is advisable to keep an
index reference of all the books that have been used in preparation for the
referencing and bibliography. There are online facilities, such as Questia
(www.questia.com), which can support this process.

Referencing and citations

A citation is a section of words quoted/copied directly from an author. It may also be indirect when the learner puts the author's ideas into their own words. It must be acknowledged that this has been done to help with the assignment and to avoid plagiarism (see Figure 3.3).

Including a quotes citation in your assignment

When writing an assignment, quotes taken from a text or information and ideas from books and other materials will need to be indicated. This can be done by writing the author's name, the publication date and page number (in brackets), and then the quote in 'inverted commas'.

Direct quote/citation copied within the text

For example: 'The Health and Safety Act of 1974 is a good starting point when looking at our duties in keeping children safe' (Tassoni, 2002: 9).
or

Indirect quote/citation summarizing within the text

For example: Tassoni (2002) suggests that the Health and Safety Act of 1974 is worth looking at, as it identifies the duties staff must take to keep children safe.

No inverted commas are used as the author's words have been summarized. A reference at the end of the piece of work provides the reader with enough details about the citations so that they can find the information and sources used. It should answer the following questions:

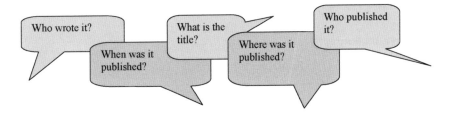

Figure 3.3 Acknowledging a citation.

All assignments require references and a bibliography to acknowledge the source of references used, such as books, articles, journals, and websites accessed to gain information. This is called a bibliography because it is the identification of books and materials used in the piece of work. It goes at the end of the work showing all the books and materials that have been used and looked at for the piece of work.

Referencing is essential because:

- It shows you have read and understood books, etc.
- It gives evidence to support any points you have made
- It tells others about materials that could be useful to them
- Your tutor can check where you got your facts from
- It can be helpful for revision before exams

As stated previously, using another person's words or ideas **without** referencing them is called **plagiarism. This is not allowed.** Most universities and colleges will use the Harvard referencing system. It is important to find out which system is being used and to adhere to it throughout.

When reading, make a note of all the following details:

- Author/editor
- Date
- Title
- Publisher
- Volume/issue number
- Pages
- URL (websites)

The Harvard system always uses an alphabetical approach starting with the author's surname and listing references in alphabetical order.

Many different books and materials may have been used in an assignment to back up what is being said. At the end of the assignment, there should be a list of all the sources. This takes the form of the references and bibliography section.

Writing a bibliography

From a book: Surname, Initial. (Date) *Title of Book*. Place: Publisher.

 e.g.   Tassoni, P. (2002) *Certificate in Childcare and Education*. Oxford: Heinemann.

More than one author: Tassoni, P. and Beith, K.
Tassoni, P. *et al.* (more than two authors)

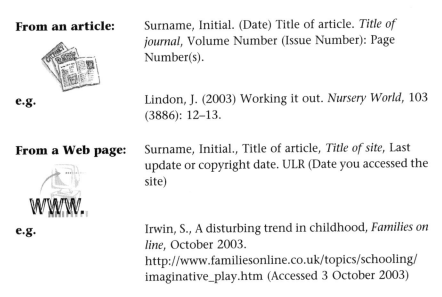

From an article: Surname, Initial. (Date) Title of article. *Title of journal*, Volume Number (Issue Number): Page Number(s).

e.g.   Lindon, J. (2003) Working it out. *Nursery World*, 103 (3886): 12–13.

From a Web page: Surname, Initial., Title of article, *Title of site*, Last update or copyright date. ULR (Date you accessed the site)

e.g.   Irwin, S., A disturbing trend in childhood, *Families on line*, October 2003. http://www.familiesonline.co.uk/topics/schooling/ imaginative_play.htm (Accessed 3 October 2003)

If information that is needed for referencing is not available, a learning resource centre's Opac (library search engine), the British Library or Copac on the internet should help find elusive information from books and articles.

Use the following checklist before handing in your finished work:

Format and Layout	Tick when checked
Times New Roman (size 12 font)	
Double spacing	
Margins on each side	
Black text and white paper unless otherwise stated	
Clear breaks between paragraphs and sections	
Title page with full title of assignment	
Name and KU number on each page as a footer (size 10 font)	
All pages numbered	
References	
Author, date and page number where appropriate. (Harvard referencing – available on Blackboard, Student Handbook)	
Internet references should clearly identify the website used and date accessed	
Pictures, diagrams, and charts need to be referenced/labelled clearly	

Language	
Avoid colloquialisms and slang	
Avoid shortened versions of words (Write 'did not' instead of 'didn't')	
Proof read carefully for minor errors	
Presentation	
Avoid plastic A4 wallets for individual sheets of paper	
Use a good A4 plastic folder, hole punch work, and include dividers for appendices	
Make two copies	

Learning styles

It is important to know how learning takes place and also to understand how children learn so that practitioners can ensure the most effective opportunities for individual children to practise and develop new skills. How can children's learning be facilitated if the practitioner is not open to new experiences?

Learning is a lifelong process. Sometimes it is enjoyable, sometimes it is painful, and sometimes it is hard work.

> What we usually mean by learning are those more or less permanent changes brought about voluntarily in one's patterns of acting, thinking and/or feelings. There are at least two parts to the process: the reception of and engagement with the material, i.e. the development of new perceptions or the engagement in new forms of activity and secondly, the response to this new material.
>
> (Rogers 2002: 86)

Learning happens when someone demonstrates something that we didn't know before. There are many different ways of looking at learning (VAK):

- Visual learners
- Auditory learners
- Kinaesthetic (practical) learners

There are many ways of ascertaining what kind of learning style a person has. VAK is one of the tests that can be used to pinpoint a person's preferred learning style. There is a huge selection of sites online. The following site is a simple and effective one:

VAK test online Jester, C. (2000)
http://www.metamath.com/lsweb/dvclearn.htm

Visual

Visual learners have a tendency to process information better when it is in a visual form such as pictorial, diagrammatic, graphic, video or written format. When in a learning environment or a learning experience, they will express themselves by saying things such as, 'I see' or 'I get the picture'. Visual learners need to see to learn, so to understand the full content of the learning experience, they will need to see a person's body language and facial expressions. Visual learners use notes, handouts, and mind maps to help them understand information.

Auditory

Auditory learners will express themselves by saying 'I hear you' or 'that sounds like a good idea'. They learn best by listening to conversations or presentations. Taking notes will probably get in the way of their learning process. Learning is best for them through oral lessons, talking things through, and listening to others.

Kinaesthetic (practical)

Kinaesthetic learners are hands-on learners who like to actively explore their physical environment. They will tend to say things like 'I feel'. Sitting down for long periods of time may be difficult for them, as abstract concepts are explained through active involvement such as building models or moving objects around.

Learning dynamics (Honey and Mumford 1992)

Dimensions

- *Theorist*: someone who thinks things through in a logical way.
- *Pragmatist*: someone who likes to try out new ideas and then put them into practice.
- *Activist*: someone who is open minded and willing to try out new ideas.
- *Reflector*: someone who will reflect on the situation before acting.

Reflective thinking

One of the skills a learner needs to develop is that of the art of reflective thinking. John Dewey (1938:118) was the first to advocate this idea in his book *Experience and Education*. He describes reflective thought within teaching and learning as the 'active, persistent and careful consideration of any belief or supposed form of knowledge in light of the grounds that supports it in the further conclusions of which it tends'. Reflective thinking is about being willing to engage in continuous self-appraisal and development to better understand the reasoning behind a concept and why that concept is held.

In childcare and education, it is good to be a reflective thinker to improve, challenge, and raise the levels of current practice. The act of writing something down brings it into conscious thought and helps to clarify these concepts and emotions. This enables strategies to be formed and provides a focus for future development and progression.

Reflective practice is about meditating, contemplating, and consciously thinking about childcare and educational practice so that change and improvement can be made. Such change will help practitioners to be better prepared to meet the needs of the children in their care, and understand the theoretical principles and ethos that informs our practice.

Are the beliefs, principles, and values that are held for childcare and education reflected in everyday practice?

Critically, analysis is necessary so that plans can be revised and provision of childcare implemented to meet the children's needs in the early years setting. This means that the practitioner will need to be open and willing critically to analyse practice, which is not always an easy thing to do. It is all about being active not passive in practice. 'The aim of reflective practice is thus to support a shift from routine actions rooted in common sense thinking to reflective action stemming from professional thinking' (Pollard and Tann 1994: 20). Key stages of the reflective process are shown in Figure 3.4.

Reflective learning log

A reflective learning log is an invaluable tool in stimulating the above process and bringing it into conscious thought. A reflective learning log will describe 'critical' aspects that have happened in everyday professional childcare and educational practice in the work setting. It will reflect analysis of these aspects, the conclusions that have been drawn, and how they have then affected thinking and future practice. It should also link to the modules that are currently studied and how this has impacted on development and practice.

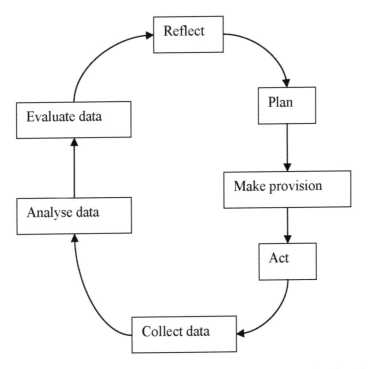

Figure 3.4 Key stages of the reflective process (reproduced with permission from Pollard and Tann 1994: 12).

The reflective process follows five steps:

1. *Detailed description.* What has happened? Describe a detailed experience, event or activity that has occurred during the day. Write down what has happened, express feelings about it and any judgements that can be made.
2. *Analysis.* What was really important about what happened? What has been learnt from the experience? Is it positive or negative? What personal learning has taken place?
3. *Interpretation.* What does it mean? How does the experience, event or activity fit into the wider context? How did it go?
4. *Judgement.* What impact has the experience had on the practitioner? What implications are there? What issues arose through completing this log?
5. *Action.* What needs to be pursued? What are the implications for future practice? What actions are going to be taken in light of what has been learnt? What are the implications of these actions?

Taken and adapted from an unpublished lecture by Jean Godber (1998)

Theorists

When being a reflective practitioner, it is important to make links between experiential learning and the underpinning theoretical implications that influence practice. There are several pioneering theorists whose ideas are still influencing the work of practitioners and theorists today (see Figure 3.5).

Theory – Behaviourist	Theory – Psychoanalytical Learning Theory	Theory – Psychoanalytical Learning Theory
B.F. Skinner	**Sigmund Freud**	**Erik Erikson**
1904–1990	1856–1939	1902–1994
USA	Czechoslovakia	Germany
Operant conditioning	Psychosexual stages of child development	Psychosocial stages of development
Key Issues • Primary reinforcement • Secondary reinforcement • Generalized reinforcement 'Skinner box'	**Key Issues** 1. Oral 2. Anal 3. Phallic 4. Latency 5. Genital Id Ego Superego	**Key Issues** 1. Basic trust vs. mistrust 2. Autonomy vs. shame and doubt 3. Initiative vs. guilt 4. Industry vs. inferiority 5. Identity vs. identity diffusion 6. Intimacy vs. isolation 7. Generativity vs. stagnation 8. Ego integrity vs. despair
Relevance to Early Years Highlights the importance of behaviour reinforcement	**Relevance to Early Years** Understanding of human development and psyche	**Relevance to Early Years** Provides a framework for the progression of healthy emotional and social development
Further Reading Cooper, S. (2005) *Learning Theories Site Map.* (http://www.lifecircles-inc.com/learningmap.htm: accessed 30 August 2007).	**Further Reading** Berk, L. (2005) *Child Development.* Cambridge: Pearson International.	**Further Reading** Berk, L. (2005) *Child Development.* Cambridge: Pearson International.

Theory – Cognitive Constructivism	Theory – Cognitive Constructivism	Theory – Cognitive Constructivism
Jean Piaget	**Jean Piaget**	**Chris Athey**
1896–1980	1896–1980	Current researcher
Switzerland	Switzerland	United Kingdom
Stages of cognitive development	Schemas	Developmental stages relating to schemas
Key Issues 1. Sensori-motor 2. Pre-operational 3. Concrete operational 4. Formal operational	**Key Issues** Two principles underlying children's schemas: 1. Assimilation 2. Accommodation Assimilation = Equilibrium New Situation = Disequilibrium leading to Accommodation	**Key Issues** 1. Motor level 2. Symbolic Representation 3. Thought level
Relevance to Early Years Understanding of cognitive development and adaptation to real- world experiences	**Relevance to Early Years** Understanding of children's categorization and mental mapping of the world around them	**Relevance to Early Years** Understanding of schemas in early years has informed observational work and planning
Further Reading Berk, L. (2005) *Child Development*. Cambridge: Pearson International.	**Further Reading** Berk, L. (2005) *Child Development*. Cambridge: Pearson International.	**Further Reading** Athey, C. (1990) *Extending Thought in Young Children*. London: Paul Chapman.
Theory – Intelligence	Theory – Socio-dramatic Play	Theory – The effects of pre-school education and care on children's development for children aged 3–7 years
Howard Gardener	**Sara Smilansky**	**Kathy Sylva**
Current researcher	Current researcher	Current researcher
USA	Israel	USA
Multiple intelligences	Socio-dramatic play	Effective provision of pre-school education project

Key Issues	Key Issues	Key Issues
1. Verbal-linguistic 2. Logical-mathematical 3. Visual-spatial 4. Body-kinaesthetic 5. Musical-rhythmic 6. Interpersonal 7. Intrapersonal	Four stages of play: 1. Functional 2. Constructive 3. Dramatic 4. Games with rules	Pre-school experience is an important foundation in children's holistic development. Duration and continuity of attendance increases the chances of improved cognitive development. Full-time provision does not offer better results for the child than part-time provision. High-quality provision has the most impact for those from a disadvantaged background. Children from a disadvantaged background attend less regularly than other groups.
Relevance to Early Years Provides a way to classify behaviour or learning pattern as intelligence. Provides understanding of the importance of genetically determined cognitive thought	**Relevance to Early Years** The play environment is important in encouraging children's learning	**Relevance to Early Years** Highlights the importance of good quality, sustainable early years' provision.
Further Reading Cooper, S. (2005) *Learning Theories Site Map.* (http://www.lifecircles-inc.com/learningmap.htm: accessed 30 August 2007).	**Further Reading** Brain, C. and Mukherji, P. (2005) *Understanding Child Psychology.* Cheltenham: Nelson Thornes.	**Further Reading** SureStart (2004) *The Effective Provision of Pre-School Education (EPPE).* London: SureStart.

Theory – Early Years Education and Play	Theory – Social Learning	Theory – Constructivism and Discovery Learning
Tina Bruce	**Lev Vygotsky**	**Jerome Bruner**
Current researcher	1896–1934	1915–
United Kingdom	Russia	USA
The 12 features of play	Zones of development	Modes of thought and stages of cognitive development
Key Issues 'Free-flow play'. 12 features of play: 1. Active process without a product 2. Intrinsically motivated 3. It enables the child to be in control without restrictions 4. This is about stimulating a child's imagination, it encourages creativity, originality, and innovation 5. It encourages reflection on a meta-cognitive level 6. Emphasizes the use of previous first-hand experiences 7. It offers preparation for real-life experiences 8. Using previous experiences to be in control. 9. It is child or adult initiated; if it is the latter, the adult needs to emphasize 3, 5, and 11 of these characteristics 10. It can involve solitary play 11. It can involve a group or joint venture with adults being sensitive to the children's needs 12. It incorporates all the things we have learnt and understand.	**Key Issues** Zone of Proximal development (ZPD) Zone of actual development (ZAD)	**Key Issues** 'Scaffolding' Enactive representation Iconic representation Symbolic representation

Relevance to Early Years	Relevance to Early Years	Relevance to Early Years
The importance of allowing children to play freely	How adults can facilitate and ameliorate children's learning to progress to a higher level than would occur if left without input	Emphasizes the adult's role in facilitating children's learning
Further Reading Bruce, T. and Meggitt, C. (1996) *Childcare and Education*. London: Hodder & Stoughton.	**Further Reading** Berk, L. (2005) *Child Development*. Cambridge: Pearson International.	**Further Reading** Jarvis, M. and Chandler, E. (2001) *Angles on Child Psychology*. Cheltenham: Nelson Thornes.
Theory – Observational Learning	Theory – Bonding and Attachment	Theory – Secure and Insecure Attachment
Albert Bandura	**John Bowlby**	**Mary Ainsworth**
1925–	1907–1990	1913–1999
Canada	United Kingdom	USA
Social learning	Separation anxiety	Categorization of secure and insecure attachment The stranger situation technique
Key Issues 'Bobo doll' Four processes involved with observing and imitating behaviour: 1. Attention processes 2. Retention processes 3. Production processes 4. Motivational processes	**Key Issues** 1. Orientation and pattern recognition 2. Secure base behaviour – 'set-goal' attachment 3. Formation of a reciprocal relationship	**Key Issues** Secure Insecure – detached Insecure – resistant Insecure – disorganized
Relevance to Early Years The importance of role modelling behaviour for children, and that children are active participants in this process. Children learn a great deal from reinforce-ment and punishment	**Relevance to Early Years** Understanding the emotional trauma that separation and bereavement can have on children	**Relevance to Early Years** The effect of separation anxiety and importance of the type of attachment they have with their main carer

Further Reading	Further Reading	Further Reading
Flanagan, C. (1996) *Applying Psychology to Early Child Development.* Oxford: Hodder & Stoughton.	Bowlby, J. (1965) *Child Care and the Growth of Love.* London: Penguin.	Bee, H. (2006) *Child Development* (11th edn.). Cambridge: Pearson International.

Figure 3.5 Pioneering theorists.

Summary

This chapter enables the practitioner to develop skills, knowledge, and understanding to provide high-quality care and provision for children through reflective practice.

The grow model emphasizes the importance of recognizing the procedure of creating change or improvement by understanding the learning process. This helps to identify future learning goals.

Learners cannot further their academic career without developing good study skills as a foundation to support their learning. One of the areas that this chapter covers is the essential skills that provide a basis for future learning and development.

Being a reflective practitioner researcher links the work of the theorists to professional and personal development, thereby reflecting on the provision provided for the children.

References

Athey, C. (1990) *Extending Thought in Young Children.* London: Paul Chapman.

Bee, H. (2006) *Child Development* (11th edn). Cambridge: Pearson International.

Berk, L. (2005) *Child Development.* Cambridge: Pearson International.

Bowlby, J. (1965) *Child Care and the Growth of Love.* London: Penguin.

Brain, C. and Mukherji, P. (2005) *Understanding Child Psychology.* Cheltenham: Nelson Thornes.

Bruce, T. and Meggitt, C. (1996) *Childcare and Education.* London: Hodder & Stoughton.

Cooper, S. (2005) *Learning Theories Site Map* (http://www.lifecirclesinc.com/learningmap.htm: accessed 30 August 2007).

Cottrell, S. (2003) *The Study Skills Handbook.* Basingstoke: Palgrave.

Dewey, J. (1933) *How We Think: A Restatement of the Relation of Reflective Thinking to the Education Process.* Boston, MA: O.C. Heath.

Flanagan, C. (1996) *Applying Psychology to Early Child Development.* Oxford: Hodder & Stoughton.

Honey, P. and Mumford, A. (1992) *The Manual of Learning Styles.* Maidenhead: Peter Honey.

Jarvis, M. and Chandler, E. (2001) *Angles on Child Psychology*. Cheltenham: Nelson Thornes.

Jester, C. (2000) *DVC Online, Introduction to the DVC Learning Style Survey for College* (http://www.metamath.com/lsweb/dvclearn.htm: accessed 26 September 2007).

Pollard, A. and Tann, S. (1994) *Reflective Teaching in Primary School*. London: Cassell.

Quality Improvement Agency (2006) *Participation Handbook; Professional Training for Subject Learning Coaches*. London: Learning Skills Development Agency.

Rogers, A. (2002) *Teaching Adults* (3rd edn). Maidenhead: Open University Press.

SureStart (2004) *The Effective Provision of Pre-School Education (EPPE)*. London: SureStart.

Truss, L. (2003) *Eats, Shoots and Leaves: The Zero Tolerance Approach to Punctuation*. London: Profile Books.

4   Ethics, beliefs, and values in early years

The engine of cultural change is the human capacity for creative thought and action.

NACCCE (1999: 6)

Sustaining a learning community and ethical research culture in a busy setting requires shared values and beliefs, open and honest dialogue, and support for developing practitioners' expertise as competent researchers. This chapter will seek to engage practitioners in identifying their own key values and beliefs within an ethical framework that can be shared with others. Ethics in this instance are seen as 'the principles of conduct governing an individual or group' (*Penguin English Dictionary* 1992).

As a practitioner, it can be difficult to know how external decisions are made (KCF Strand 1). Statutory requirements on issues such as health and safety (The Early Years Foundation Stage) and safeguarding children (Childcare Act 2006) are acknowledged with the ongoing development of policies and procedures. Ownership is enhanced as those involved within a setting are actively engaged in the process of developing the policies (KCF Strand 3).

Government guidelines for practice are based on a pre-agreed set of principles that have been evolving for early years since the late 1990s (QCA 2000; SureStart 2003; DfES 2005; DCSF 2007). These can encourage individuals and groups to develop quality early years practice within their own context when not just taken as prescriptive. Increasingly, practitioners have to adopt or adapt new procedures, making decisions at a rapid pace with or without supporting evidence from research. When making quick decisions, individuals draw on in-built values and beliefs that they assume will benefit those concerned.

The focus, for once, is on the practitioner as well as the child. The links between values, beliefs, and ethics will be discussed using a framework that has been selected to explore the values evident within the ethical background that work-based practitioner learners currently engage in. Rowson (2006) developed a framework for looking at 'working ethics', which has been adapted to facilitate raising awareness and discussion. The framework uses the mnemonic FAIR to remember the four key values – Fairness, Autonomy, Integrity, and Results of practice – which are aimed at enhancing working environments and reducing potential for harm (Figure 4.1). Links within and across areas will be made to the Key Components Framework (KCF) strands.

Inevitably, ethical dilemmas will continue to occur in practice, requiring practitioners who are willing and able to debate and seek ethical conclusions. This tension, if used constructively, can strengthen a learning community and research culture.

Personal philosophies, values, and beliefs

How do we see ourselves in relation to others – colleagues, peers, parents, children, and the wider society? Reflective practice provides opportunities continuously to visit our image of self within the work context, and as this happens there is the potential to look deeper at events that have influenced the way we respond to situations and to question the way we responded.

A personal journal allows space to note down individual beliefs and values that may appear too personal to discuss with others but may help identify why we feel strongly about certain issues, sometimes causing conflict with others (KCF Strand 2). Over a period of time, certain concerns may return, identifying the importance of a specific issue. Each work-based practitioner learner has built and continues to build up values from family, surrounding cultural, educational, and life experiences, some of which may be more consciously identifiable than others. They may only come into question when an incident occurs that can lead to a surprising conflict between two parties, opening up hitherto unknown differences in long-held values. An ethical framework can provide a non-threatening tool to reflect on and discuss potential incidents, sharing ways to manage these while allowing for differences. This facilitates separation of the issue or concern from those who hold differing values, thus preventing a destructive 'blame' culture emerging.

> *Pause for thought*: Who in your workplace knows how valuable a close family relationship is to you? Is there a set of circumstances that could arise where it could be beneficial for others to know?

Similarly, beliefs held by individuals may be rarely verbalized on a day-to-day basis. Work-based practice is likely to demonstrate the impact of one's beliefs on daily living but use of a 'common spiritual language' leading to sharing and discussion of beliefs may be limited. Personalized beliefs may or may not fit into generic expectations of the behaviour or customs of one of the major religions. Sometimes beliefs – and values – may have been adopted without conscious individual choice and may only be identified when a key issue arises. A reflective journal kept over a period of time may provide an opportunity to explore this further.

Pause for thought: Who in your workplace knows whether you believe in God? Is there a set of circumstances that could arise where it could be beneficial for others to know?

Values and beliefs are held and portrayed within an individual personality (see Chapter 1). An ethical framework allows common ground to be identified in a way that helps daily management of a society, in this instance a work-based setting. The following FAIR model was developed by philosopher Richard Rowson while working with different disciplines, so it would appear viable for the increasingly multi-professional work of the early years work-based practitioner learner. The principles used here can be linked directly to those underpinning the five outcomes of *Every Child Matters: Change for Children* (DfES 2003) and in the *Early Years Foundation Stage* (0–5 years) (DCSF 2007).

In 1954, Piaget's seminal work on children's cognitive development raised awareness of how babies begin to 'construct reality'. Since then, many researchers, practitioners, psychologists, and neuroscientists have begun to explore the possibilities of a 'theory of mind'. Understanding desires, emotions, and beliefs can play an important role in social interactions. Eventually, children come to realize that other people can have a different belief to their own. The Sally-Anne false belief task (Wimmer and Perner 1983) tests children's 'theory of mind' by presenting scenarios that require children to problem solve a simple situation relating to object permanence.

Frith (1992) repeated the experiment with human actors (rather than dolls) and found similar results. More recently, two further studies by Malinda Carpenter, Josep Call, and Michael Tomasello (2002) found that 36-month-old children can understand others' false beliefs. Cumulative data, ethically documented over a period of time, can push the boundaries of knowledge and understanding further to give the best and most appropriate results in the current social context.

The values demonstrated in the FAIR model will enable professionals to:

- work effectively within culturally complex democracies;
- earn the trust of people using their services;
- be mutually supportive of the work of other professions;
- promote democratic ideals;
- be fair in the treatment of people of different cultures.

(Rowson 2006: 14)

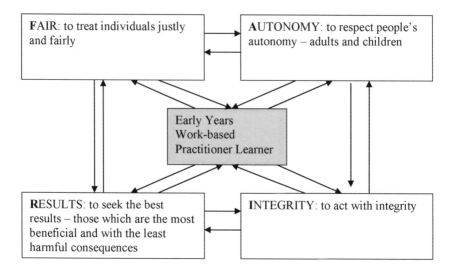

Figure 4.1 The framework for ethical thinking in the professions (adapted from Rowson 2006: 151).

Activity: Rowson's 'Ethical Framework for Thinking in the Professions'

Two different dimensions to exploring the ethical framework. (This activity may be carried out individually or in small groups.) For each of the four boxes, write down examples drawn from your practice which relate to:

(a) yourself as a work-based practitioner learner – such as ways you are treated fairly within your learning group, examples of your own autonomy within your setting, acknowledgement of your integrity . . .

(b) your impact on others – such as specific examples of your own fair practice in relation to colleagues, parents or children, ways you encourage autonomy for others, use of your integrity in decision making . . .

These examples can be revisited after exploring each aspect in more detail.

Although each area of Rowson's framework can be used, inevitably there will be links between them as acknowledged within the model. Also there is no priority in the order of presentation.

Fair: to treat individuals (adults and children) justly and fairly

Early years practitioners will be familiar with key legislation relating to equal opportunities – Children Act (DfEE 1989), Racial Discrimination Act (DfEE 2004), and the Disability Discrimination Act (DfEE 2006). The ethical framework above can be used to promote debate about practice where tension arises over what is considered 'fair' and 'just'. As practitioners study and share their practice together, inevitable comparisons are made with regard to available resources, roles, and responsibilities.

Pause for thought:

- What is 'fair' when it comes to looking at the differing range of outdoor provision? Now a requirement for early years practice (Early Years Foundation Stage 2007), has the national recommendation made access to outdoor play fairer for all?
- What is 'just' about when a child with a physical disability has to travel to a day-care setting in a different area to gain the required care?

List some questions arising from your own practice about what is 'fair' and/or 'just'?

The ethos of a setting can demonstrate ownership of the value of fairness. Dahlberg and Moss (2005) talk about creating a sense of responsibility and respect for 'otherness'. This looks beyond issues of children's rights (UNCRC 1989; The Children Act 1989, 2004) to view children and adults as active participants in an 'ethics of an encounter'. This, by its nature, moves towards fairness and justice as it seeks to give individuals within the setting community a voice. The 'other' within this debate seeks to make sure that we really are not trying to make others images of ourselves, or what we understand others should be. A 'pedagogy of listening' (Rinaldi, cited in Dahlberg and Moss 2005: 97) is essential in giving children a voice in this chapter.

Conflict resolution techniques, strategies, and skills used within a setting can also work towards fairness and justice. They are underpinned by effective communication skills and the ability to cooperate, collaborate, and communicate. The challenge here is to allow for opportunities to develop these skills through practice, understanding that they are skills that are learnt. Time needs to be allowed for individuals and groups – adults and children together – to have 'encounters', to get to know and trust each other, and create their own ground rules for fairness and justice. The process also acknowledges diversity and should be an example of inclusive practice.

Working with other professionals, whether multi-agency or multi-disciplinary, can support the values of fairness and justice by, for example, acknowledging that at times additional support and advice is needed. Miller *et al.* (2005: 9) acknowledge that individuals tend to bring with them the values of their own background profession in regard to teamwork, which can influence the dynamic working of a multi-disciplinary team. As groups form, opportunities to develop a shared value base, formally and informally, will require time and sensitivity, yet may help progression of the tasks in hand.

Observation, assessment monitoring, recording, planning, and evaluating can be viewed as fulfilling government requirements – 'disciplinary power' (Foucault, cited in Moss and Dahlberg 2005) or as a means to meet fairly the diverse needs of each child, identifying, addressing, and valuing their achievements.

The way change is managed within a setting can also be considered against the ethical framework:

- Is there 'justice' in terms of the changes being fitting for the particular setting at this specific time?
- Is there 'fairness' in terms of comparing the benefits for all concerned?

Activity: Use the two questions above in relation to a recent change that has occurred in your setting. How does the change appear when considered against the ethical framework (include autonomy, integrity, and results)?

Like change, the way time is managed in the workplace can also have implications for fairness and justice. Decisions need to be made about such issues as rotas and timetabling. How do the values of fairness and justice impact on work-based practice and learning here? This is especially pertinent to children's centres where qualified teaching staff share working hours according to their teaching contract, whereas non-qualified teaching staff may be on a lower salary and less attractive pension yet work similar hours, for example a practitioner with early years professional status.

Opportunities for the voice of the child and the voice of the adult to be heard will demonstrate the pedagogy of listening and the development of 'ethics of an encounter', acknowledging the value of fairness. There is then the requirement for appropriate action, linking to the other three aspects of the framework.

Autonomy and respect for children and their views

The United Nations Convention on the Rights of the Child (UNICEF 1989) contains four key principles:

- non-discrimination;
- devotion to the best interests of the child;

- the right to life, survival, and development; and
- respect for the views of the child.

The Convention protects children's rights by setting standards in health care, education, legal, civil, and social services. Currently, many researchers of young children are from a multi-agency background. However, they are often not part of the learning community they are researching. The British Education Research Association (BERA) has revised its ethical guidelines, which builds on the 1992 statement to recognize:

> Firstly, the academic tensions that a multi-disciplinary community generates when dealing with the complex research issues that characterise education contexts and secondly, it seeks to include the field of action research. The principles underpinning the guidelines are that all educational research should be conducted with an ethic of respect for:
>
> ○ the Person;
> ○ knowledge;
> ○ democratic Values;
> ○ the Quality of Educational Research;
> ○ academic Freedom.
>
> In guiding researchers on their conduct within this framework the Association sets out its guidelines under the following headings:
>
> ○ responsibilities to participants;
> ○ responsibilities to Sponsors of Research;
> ○ responsibilities to the Community of Educational Researchers.
> (BERA 2004: 5)

To acknowledge that practitioners may be working with young and vulnerable children, the British Education Research Association asks that researchers comply with Articles 3 and 12 of the UN Convention on the Rights of the Child. Article 3 in particular requires that all actions concerning children should be in the best interests of the child and that they must be the primary consideration. Article 12 relates to giving children a 'voice', in that children who are capable of forming their own views should be granted the right to express them.

Practitioners working in settings during their foundation degree or BA (Hons) degree have a duty of care to ensure that the principles and guidelines above are recognized and implemented. In my experience, practitioners studying early years in the workplace have often bypassed the principles and headed straight to the guidelines for practice. The new Early Years Foundation

Stage (DCSF 2007) has reduced the principles from ten to four, which are directly linked to the *Every Child Matters* (DfES 2003) outcomes:

- *A unique child* – recognizes that every child is a competent learner from birth who can be resilient, capable, confident, and self-assured. The commitments are focused around development, inclusion, safety, health, and well-being.
- *Positive relationships* – describes how children learn to be strong and independent from a base of a loving and secure relationship with parents and/or key person. The commitments are focused around respect, partnership with parents, supporting learning, and the role of the key person.
- *Enabling environments* – explains that the environment plays a key role in supporting and extending children's developing learning. The commitments are focused around observation; assessment and planning; support for every child; the learning environment and the wider context – transition, continuity, and multi-agency working.
- *Learning and development* – recognizes that children develop and learn in different ways and at different rates, and that all areas of learning and development are equally important and interconnected (DCSF 2007).

Why we need ethical principles

The principles expressed in the Early Years Foundation Stage (DCSF 2007) have inherent values, which are an essential ingredient to the role of the early years professional. In a time of rapid change in the sector, having an enabling set of principles can underpin the development of setting policies and procedures. For example, it can offer opportunities for discussion to 'think through' a policy *before* writing and implementing it.

Questions:

- Does outdoor learning seek the best results – treat girls, boys, and staff fairly, provide respect for their autonomy, and enable them all to act with integrity?
- How do the health and safety aspects of an outdoor educational visit seek the best results – treat girls, boys, and staff fairly, provide respect for their autonomy, and enable them all to act with integrity?

Enabling children to have a voice when undertaking practitioner research has its drawbacks. The practitioner may be working in a setting that takes children from birth to five years. This can mean that the practitioner must recognize and have responsibility to address a wider community, including parents. According to Robinson and Kellet (2004: 85), 'the ways in which researchers view children are pivotal to the power relations that ensue between researcher and participant'. They put forward Christensen and Prout's (cited in Robinson and Kellett 2004: 85) four ways of approaching childhood research by thinking about the following:

- child as an object;
- child as a subject;
- child as a social actor; and
- child as a participant co-researcher.

Researchers must also recognize that owing to the vulnerability issues relating to babies and young children, they should be rigorous not only about ethical aspects, but also the appropriateness of the complete research process.

There are now acknowledged multi-modal ways forward for engaging children to elicit their views and opinions. Alison Clark (2004) uses what is termed the 'mosaic approach', which encompasses a range of methods to gain as wide a picture of children's views and daily lives as possible. Clark uses a variety of methods for collecting data, including observations, child conferencing, cameras, tours, map making, and interviews. She also takes a stance that puts the researcher in an 'inexpert' position and the child as an 'expert'. Clark's work has been influenced by the pedagogical approaches used in Reggio Emilia (Italy) whereby the child is considered to be a competent learner, able to communicate verbally and non-verbally.

Learning stories also use many ways of documenting children's belief in their own abilities, such as using pictures, digital photos, and camcorders to enable children to document their own stories. Carr (2001) agues that formative assessment where children and their families are included can encourage all to reflect so as to extend data and information. This in turn encourages a child's self-belief as well as supporting parents and carers to be well informed of their child's progress and achievements.

Anne Smith (2007) writes:

> In my view, it is a responsibility for researchers, professionals and agencies working for children (including practitioners) to keep governments honest and insist they fulfil the promises they made when they implemented the Convention of Human Rights.

Results: to seek the best results – those which are the most beneficial and with the least harmful consequences for all.

The above ethical statement has always been key to practice in health and social care and will also be clearly identifiable within early years principles for effective practice, the provision of care, and learning opportunities. There are close links to fairness and justice for adults and children.

Seedhouse (cited in Katz *et al.* 2000: 103) developed an ethical grid to help practitioners in health reflect on specific situations. The 'best results' were outcomes that not only related to oneself, but also the 'patient', the particular group, and society. This acknowledges the enormity of the ethical debate, allowing for ongoing exploration for the early years practitioners. For early years practitioners, replace the word 'patient' with child.

Identification of a specific 'ethics of care' can also link with early years practice:

> the moral agent in the ethics of care, stands with both feet in the real world . . . The ethics of care demands reflection on the best course of action in specific circumstances and the best way to express and interpret moral problems.
>
> (Sevenhuijsen, cited in Dahlberg and Moss 2005: 75)

This is a reminder of the moral and hence ethical implications that come with the daily care routines carried out within settings. Maybe, justifiably, statutory guidelines are followed in areas such as staff ratios to limit potential damage or harm. These are the occasions when working with 'disciplinary power' from above may be appreciated, but is time allowed for individuals to feel empowered through their use?

Responsibilities for results can be seen to lie with senior management at times, but as Sevenhuijsen implies above, ongoing care is an everyday reality. Use of the practitioner's increasing knowledge of child development, backed by ongoing practitioner research, can mean that 'best results' for practice are open to change. This ties in with the implication of the word 'seek' in the framework. Any results are not set in stone and are best considered in context. The practitioner has the opportunity to share examples of best practice as well as concerns about possible harmful consequences with peers and colleagues, opening up debate within the learning community. Practitioner work-based research allows for the collection of evidence that acknowledges difficulties as well as achievements.

Integrity

Researchers' responsibilities include keeping intact and protecting the integrity of research by ensuring that they do not bring it into disrepute. Researchers must:

> Accord due respect to all methodologies and related methods. They must contribute to the community spirit of critical analysis and constructive criticism that generates improvement in practice and enhancement of knowledge.
>
> (BERA 2004)

It is often the case that research of any kind of will raise further questions. Practitioner research is sometimes called practitioner enquiry and stems from action research. Practitioner research within work-based learning focuses on how a practitioner can inform practice with academic activities while maintaining and supporting children, families, and the setting's needs.

Chris Smith, the then Secretary of State for Culture, Media, and Sport, wrote in *All Our Futures* (NACCCE 1999):

> The opportunities to explore the best of contemporary culture and to express individual creativity are two vital components of any education system committed to developing the full potential of all its pupils. They also play an essential role in nurturing a lively society and dynamic economy.

There are many assumptions in this statement, such as are children being 'prepared for the future' or should they be considered as participant 'players' in everyday life with their own ideas and creativity being valued for who they are? There is general agreement among researchers that any research that includes children should take place in the social context of their lives and also take into account their ideas to give as full a picture as possible.

UNESCO's action in special educational needs has been set up explicitly within the 'inclusive education' framework adopted at the Salamanca Conference in 1994. This framework stems from the Jomtien World Declaration on Education for All (1990). Concurrently, 'inclusive education' is an issue that cuts across all education initiatives – from early childhood to primary education, vocational education, adult education, teacher education, and curriculum development, as well as in spheres related to culture and social development.

The Equality Act (2006) was passed to establish the Commission for Equality and Human Rights (CEHR), which replaced the Commission for Race

Equality, Equal Opportunities Commission, and the Disability Rights. It is concerned to make:

> Discrimination unlawful on the grounds of religion or belief in the provision of goods, facilities and services, the disposal and management of premises, education, and the exercise of public functions. To create a duty on public authorities to promote equality of opportunity between men and women, and to prohibit sex discrimination in the exercise of public functions.
>
> (HM Government 2006)

The government's Inclusion Index rests on three levels:

- creating inclusive cultures;
- producing inclusive policies; and
- evolving inclusive practices.

The 'early years' of childhood are internationally recognized as being from birth to eight years; however, in the current climate of research, most focuses on children aged between three and six years. It was pointed out by an OECD research committee in 2001 that 'this could give the impression that children under the age of three are educationally unimportant'.

Part of the difficulty of research in this area is that different disciplines are involved and have their own 'codes' or terms; for example, psychologists refer to the age group from birth to three years as infants and take quite a narrow view, whereas Lesley Abbott wanted to take a much broader and inclusive approach to that age range when developing the 'Birth to Three Matters' (DfES 2002) documents.

The Special Interest Group of the British Education Research Association is mainly concerned with research in the younger age range from birth to eight. The group is particularly interested in:

- pedagogy;
- curriculum;
- adult roles, professional development, training, and the workforce.

The Special Interest Group decided to define its area by following a process that charts identified sources, which is useful for ensuring that any body of research data on a specifically chosen area keeps its integrity. For example, it should have:

- external validity;
- be based on a design that minimizes bias; and
- is germane to the issue being reviewed.

However, there are many instances where types of data can influence results, such as reference to unpublished work, emerging good practice, and articles from professional journals where the research process is implicit.

Confidentiality is a concern for all practitioners and researchers in general. It is an obvious statement to make that if one is to share the results of an investigation, then one needs to share findings. If a practitioner is transparent about his or her project/assignment from the start, then there is less chance of there being a difficulty. It is not good enough to say 'I am doing a piece of practitioner research for my degree, will you please allow me do some work with your children?' Permission needs to be sought from all parties long before any data collection. Some data may already be in the public domain, such as an OfSTED Report on the setting. However, before it is used it is essential that the manager, head teacher, and staff know it is going to be used. Children's and parents' or carers' views might also be collected if appropriate. Most practitioners know that children should not be recognizable if a photograph is used to demonstrate a child performing an activity. Many settings use a 'blanket' permission form for photographs when children enter a setting, but this is mainly to communicate with parents/carers about activities that take place during the child's day at the setting. Using a photograph, even if it has been made unrecognizable, may present difficulties ethically as it is now going out of the setting into another institution and being used for a different purpose. Confidentiality is also closely linked to privacy and therefore needs careful consideration. These problems can be overcome but do need thinking through before embarking on a research topic.

Defining an area to research is the first important step in sorting out what the title might be. Reading current research will help to identify the chosen area in terms of planning. Once a decision is made and it is going to be, for example, 'pedagogy' based, the first thing to do is define what is meant by the term. Pedagogy can have different connotations. Siraj-Blatchford *et al.* (2002: 12) suggest that pedagogy is both 'teaching and the provision of instructive learning environments and routines'. This is quite broad and reminds us to widen keyword searches, which helps with developing a research question.

Policy and pedagogical practice

The First Report of the House of Commons Education and Employment Committee, 'Early Years', was published in December 2000. This report set out areas that may be interesting to consider from the perspective of a practitioner. The report examined:

- the appropriate content of early years education;
- the way it should be taught;

- the kind of staff needed to teach and the qualifications they should have; and
- the way quality of teaching and learning in the early years is assessed and the age formal schooling should start.

When looking at pedagogy and practice, there is still much controversy about when children should begin more formal education. The 1870 Education Act first established five years as the official age for starting school. More recently, children have been entering school at the beginning of the term when they are five or even before. There have been many high-profile reports as well as comparative studies that have suggested that starting school too early can have detrimental effects, most notably the Channel 4 *Dispatches* documentary covering the work of Mills and Mills (1998) on 'Britain's Early Years'. This research considered brain development and its relevance to early years sensory and emotional development and the type of early years experiences that best suit a developing child's needs.

This debate is ongoing and it is important as individuals within a learning research community to engage in exploring issues surrounding the ethics as well as the appropriateness of any statute. It is through networking, practitioner research, demonstrating, and sharing good practice that the voices of early years workers, children, families, and the wider community will be heard and listened to (KCF Strand 2).

A recent article quotes Professor Kathy Sylva and Professor Iram Siraj-Blachford responding to the heated debate about the Early Years Foundation Stage Curriculum, scheduled to become law in September 2008, as 'far from perfect . . . but let us not abandon a largely excellent document in favour of non-regulation and lack of entitlement to high quality services' (*Times Educational Supplement*, 15 February 2008, p. 26).

References

British Education Research Association (2004) *Revised Ethical Guidelines for Educational Research*. London: BERA.

Carpenter, M., Call, J. and Tomasello, M. (2002) A new false belief test for the 36-month-olds, *British Journal of Developmental Psychology*, 20: 393–420.

Carr, M. (2001) *Assessment in Early Childhood Settings: Learning Stories*. London: Paul Chapman.

Christensen, P. and Prout, A. (2004) in S. Fraser *et al.* (eds) *Doing Research with Children and Young People*. London: Sage Publications in association with Open University Press.

Clark, A. (2004) The mosaic approach and research with young children, in V.

Lewis, M. Kellett, C. Robinson, S. Fraser and S. Ding (eds) *The Reality of Research with Children and Young People*. London: Sage.

Dahlberg, G. and Moss, P. (2005) *Ethics and Politics in Early Childhood Education*. London: Routledge Falmer.

Department for Children, Schools and Families (2007) *Early Years Foundation Stage*. London: DCSF.

Department for Education and Employment (1989) *The Children Act*. London: DfEE.

Department for Education and Employment (2004) *Racial Discrimination Act*. London: DfEE.

Department for Education and Employment (2006) *Disability Discrimination Act*. London: DfEE.

Department for Education and Skills (2002) *Birth to Three Matters: A Framework to Support Children in their Earliest Years*. London: DfES.

Department of Education and Skills (2003) *Every Child Matters: Change for Children*. London: DfES.

Department of Education and Skills (2005) *Key Elements of Effective Practice*. London: DfES.

Frith, U. (1992) *Autism: Explaining the Enigma*. Oxford: Blackwell.

HM Government of Great Britain (2006) *The Equality Act*. London: HMSO.

House of Commons Education and Employment Committee (2000) *First Report: Early Years* (http://www.publications.parliament.uk/pa/cm200001/cmselect/Cmeduemp/33/3307.htm: accessed 22 May 2008).

Katz, J., Peberdy, A. and Douglas, J. (eds) (2000) *Promoting Health: Knowledge and Practice* (2nd edn.). Oxford: The Open University.

Miller, L., Cable, C. and Devereux, J. (2005) *Developing Early Years Practice*. London: David Fulton.

Mills, C. and Mills, D. (1998) *Britain's Early Years*. London: Channel 4 Television.

National Advisory Committee on Creative and Cultural Education (1999) *All Our Futures: Creativity, Culture and Education*. London: NACCCE.

Organization for Economic Cooperation and Development (2001) *Starting Strong: Early Childhood Education and Care*. Paris: OECD.

Piaget, J. (1954) *Intelligence and Affectivity: Their Relationship during Child Development*. Palo Alto, CA: Annual Review, Inc.

Qualifications and Curriculum Authority (2000) *Curriculum Guidance for the Foundation Stage*. London: QCA.

Robinson, C. and Kellett, M. (2004) Power, in S. Fraser, V. Lewis, S. Ding, M. Kellett and C. Robinson (eds) *Doing Research with Children and Young People*. London: Sage.

Rowson, R. (2006) *The Framework for Ethical Thinking in the Professions*. London: Jessica Kingsley.

Siraj-Blatchford, I., Sylva, K., Muttock, S., Gilden, R. and Bell, D. (2002) *Researching Effective Pedagogy in the Early Years*. London: University of London Institute of Education.

Smith, A. (2007) *Children's Rights and Early Childhood Education* (http://www.earlychildhoodaustralia.org: accessed 12 October 2007).

SureStart (2003) *Birth to Three Matters*. London: DfES.

UNICEF (1989) *United Nations Convention on the Rights of the Child*. New York: UNICEF.

Wimmer, H. and Perner, J. (1983) Beliefs about beliefs: representation and constraining function of wrong beliefs in young children's understanding of deception, *Cognition*, 13: 103–28.

5 Working with others: identifying and extending a professional and personal baseline

To accomplish great things we must
first dream, then visualise, then
plan . . . believe . . . act.

Alfred A. Montapert

The ability to communicate effectively and share ideas, resources, and experiences is essential if policy and practice are to be developed further, especially in multi-agency working. Improving the welfare of and safeguarding children and opening up opportunities to enable the full potential of children and young people from 0 to 19 years is a global as well as local concern and is a central tenet of current government policy in England. The 'Every Child Matters' (DfES 2003) agenda articulates the importance of reframing services, improving integration, and developing a new, creative, and inspirational children's workforce that can communicate across the boundaries of education, health, the youth justice system, and social care. Although the nature of this proposed service and workforce re-formation is not yet in place in all local authorities, there are still many vulnerable children living in poverty, so the case and pressure for change are compelling. However, it is also complex, challenging, and can be controversial.

> Multi-agency working has been shown to be an effective way of supporting children and young people with additional needs, and securing real improvements in their life outcomes.
> (www.everychild matters.gov.uk; accessed 11 October 2007)

Different disciplines and agencies work with their own interpretations, language, and traditions and in the past most have worked to their own training schedules. Some of the overarching agencies have worked discretely, making it difficult to share expertise and experience. Time set aside for speaking, listening, and developing a shared language and understanding by practitioners cannot be underestimated as a way of moving developments forward. However, this type of extended discussion is often difficult to achieve in a busy setting environment but can be facilitated on a longer award-bearing course such as the foundation degree. Settings are normally open all year round. Therefore, it becomes even more crucial to build a learning community that makes space and time for deeper discussions.

The early years sector is in the early stages of demonstrating collaboration in practice. Any transition, whether it is a new curriculum, growing up or moving from further to higher education also includes personal life issues as well as professional ones. Work-based learning takes place within the context of our own personal and professional experiences and culture. For example, over the past five years at Kingston University, we have encountered mature work-based learners who have changed their roles and responsibilities, opened their own nurseries, married and divorced, had babies, life-threatening illnesses, and bereavements of close relatives (Key Components Framework Strand 2). There is also the issue for work-based learners of 'best fit' – that is, how the course and its requirements integrate with the reality of work-based practice in a climate of rapid change.

Having looked at the early years sector in previous chapters and the changes taking place, it is now time to examine how a professional and personal baseline can be established to enhance learning within a multi-professional context. Early years practitioners are in contact in their settings with many people from a range of disciplines and agencies as well as the community in which they work. Many agencies have acronyms, such as DIUS, which is the new Department for Innovations, Universities, and Skills. Over time, nomenclature changes and it is important to understand not just the change of name, but what that change means in terms of strategy, content, and impact in the workplace. One example of this is that the Children Act 2004 transferred responsibilities from local education authorities to the children's services authorities. However, the term 'local authority' rather than 'children's services authority' is often used to reflect this move. In terms of strategy, this has huge implications for funding, training, and changes in roles and responsibilities (KCF Strand 1).

Local authorities are increasingly using their role in early years education through community governance and leadership. The ten-year Strategy for Childcare (DfES 2004b) and the Childcare Act 2006 require local authorities to take on a number of new activities within early years and childcare:

> The main need is for local authorities to focus on the long-term delivery of reliable, consistent childcare services to families and children, taking a holistic view of the childcare market, to ensure a self-supporting, cost effective market that efficiently meets the needs of

Test your current nomenclature knowledge and give the full titles to the following:		
SpLD	OfSTED	PCT
CHAI	PRU	EP
CME	SENDA	SENDIST
BEST	SENCO	OT
EWO	DCSF	CWDC
HV	DIUS	HE
HLTA	LP	EYFS
EYPS	NFS	CAF

> parents. LAs [local authorities] should consult the private and voluntary sector providers fully when assessing supply and demand; avoid duplicating services and make maximum use of good local providers. As part of the Childcare Act 2006, local authorities will have a duty to provide information, advice and training, free of charge to local authorities and providers via the SureStart website. (DfES 2006b)

Keeping up to date with strategy that affects the practitioner is a major concern and has an impact on how the setting works in its partnership with the local authority. 'A "partnership culture" requires new ways of working and new perceptions on roles and responsibility' (DfES 2004d).

'New ways' require joined-up thinking to maximize all the identified strategies that currently work in practice to nurture and expand good practice. It is essential that practitioners are careful to have knowledge of who is responsible to whom. Specific knowledge and understanding of the boundaries and overlaps that exist between one agency/disciplinary area and another is important to ensure collaborative working. To support this move, the Children's Workforce Development Council (2007) made the following statement:

> The common core of skills, knowledge and competence would support the development of more effective and integrated services, introduce a common language amongst professionals and support staff, so starting the process of breaking down some of the cultural and practice barriers within the children's workforce: and – allied to a single framework of qualifications – promote more flexible development and career progression within the children's workforce.

The Common Core of Skills and Knowledge for the Children's Workforce (2005) and its six main headings are emebedded throughout this book.

The Childcare Act 2006

The Children Act 2004 provides the legal strength for implementing 'Every Child Matters' (DfES 2003). The new Childcare Act, passed into law on 11 July 2006, and is the first Act to be concerned exclusively with early years and childcare and provides the legislation to put the ten-year national strategy into law. Many of the early years strategies are not new but they have been strengthened or brought closer together by these two pieces of government legislation.

'Change for Children' (DfES 2004a) covers the 0 to 19 years age range and has impacted on early years provision in crucial ways. For example, the national childcare strategy focuses on the all-important five outcomes in relation to 'Early Change Matters'. 'Change for Children' is to be delivered by the top tier local authorities in England and this should be done primarily through organizational change.

The vision for the future is to create a joined-up system of multi-agency working with health, family support, childcare, and education services to ensure that there is enough provision for children, young people, and their families. It should be of high quality and include the 'child's voice' as well as those of young people and their families as to how those services will be provided. For the practitioner, this has meant that early years provision, including SureStart local programmes, have come under local authority (previously early years development and childcare partnerships) control.

> The Act will help transform childcare and early years services in England . . . these duties will require authorities to improve the five ECM ['Early Change Matters'] outcomes for all pre-school children and reduce inequalities in these outcomes; secure sufficient childcare for working parents and provide a better parental information service.
>
> (SureStart 2006)

The Childcare Act 2006 has four major sections:

1. Duties on local authorities to promote and establish different agencies and disciplines to work together to improve the five outcomes.
2. Regulation and inspection arrangements for childcare providers in England.
3. General provision for childcare.
4. Key provisions, including the collection of information about young children to inform funding and support local authority duties under the Act.

The Common Assessment Framework

The Common Assessment Framework (CAF) is a catalyst for multi-professional, multi-agency working.

> Where a child or young person with multiple additional needs requires support from more than one practitioner, the Lead Professional is someone who:
>
> ○ acts as a single point of contact that the child or young person and their family can trust, and who is able to support them in making choices and in navigating their way through the system
> ○ ensures that they get appropriate interventions when needed, which are well planned, regularly reviewed and effectively delivered
> ○ reduces overlap and inconsistency from other practitioners.
>
> (DfES 2004a)

It is understood that the lead professional will implement the Common Assessment Framework to determine the support requirements of the child or their family. The Common Assessment Framework was introduced by the Department for Education and Skills as a preventative measure to identify specific needs early and to plan for appropriate intervention rather than waiting for difficulties to arise before addressing them. The framework was designed to be used by all agencies involved with the child or family to improve the sharing and transfer of information between professionals.

The Common Assessment Framework is an example of how agencies and professionals should work together, using a common and shared language to improve the lives of children and their families. It is seen as a tool for identifying what and where support is needed, and how it will be given. The overarching message of the Common Assessment Framework is to establish mutually respectful relationships between professionals, agencies, and parents for the benefit of children.

Early years practitioners may well become the lead professional and implement the Common Assessment Framework. They will need to understand the roles and responsibilities of other professionals, have the ability to identify potential needs, and have the knowledge and skills to work collaboratively with others to improve the outcomes for the children and families under their guidance.

The Special Educational Needs and Disability Act 2001 amended the

Special Educational Needs Framework set out in the Education Act 1996, and extended the Disability Discrimination Act 1995 to include and cover provision in schools and early years settings. This is supported by the latest document entitled Implementing the Disability Discrimination Act in Schools and Early Years Settings (DfES 2006a).

In terms of the private, voluntary, and independent settings that are not part of a maintained school, settings are required not to treat disabled children less favourably and to make 'reasonable adjustments' for disabled children (IDA 1995, Part 3).

Working within an integrated framework

Working within an integrated framework requires people to work in multi-agency teams to provide specialist advice and guidance to children, young people, and families on aspects of health, social welfare, and employment (Figure 5.1). Some roles and responsibilities are yet to be designated depending on how far local authorities have established new ways of working. Use the following activity to check your knowledge of your own and others' responsibilities in this climate of change.

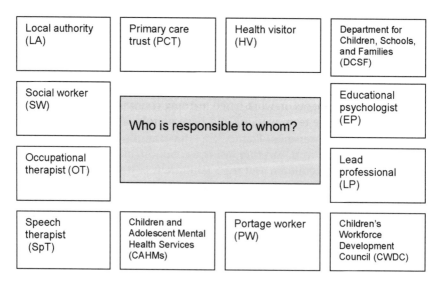

Figure 5.1 Integrated services – roles and responsibilities.

Activity

- What is the primary role of these professionals, agencies, and government departments?
- What are their responsibilities?
- Who are they accountable to?
- How is their work monitored?
- List what particular skills these professionals demonstrate and how these are continually developed.
- What are the boundaries?
- Where are the overlaps?
- Who are you accountable to?

Some useful definitions can be found in Appendix 1.

Finding ways forward for inter-professional, inter-agency working

Lessons can be learned from other disciplines, including healthcare. In 1995, the UK Centre for the Advancement of Interprofessional Education commissioned research into 'shared learning' on full-time healthcare courses. Three research papers concluded that 'shared learning' predisposed participants towards collaborative practice. However, once the practitioners completed their course and they were out in the field working, the traditions and culture of each discipline tended to reduce the improvements in collaborative working rather than extend them.

> If they [students on work-based learning courses] are not involved in collaborative team working and have no role models from which to learn, then their preparation in higher education falls on barren ground. Our research suggests that *there is a further gap between the National Health Service (NHS) trusts' concern to achieve effective team working and achieving it in practice.* No matter how supportive of multi professional education working becomes, it would be dealing with only half of the equation if a student were then faced with a culture that is hostile to the pursuit of such practice.
>
> (Miller *et al.* 2001: 225; emphasis in original)

Practitioners have the opportunity to reverse this conclusion by keeping an open mind, using a framework for talking and thinking through an issue, and making a conscious decision to learn with and from others in their academic institution and their place of work. Nothing is insurmountable, possibilities can always be created, but it does require a working environment that depends on positive relationships, a willingness to listen and empathize, and a will to work together to resolve difficulties.

This sometimes requires the practitioner consciously to draw on the hidden skills that support the Key Components Framework – for example, knowing when to negotiate, mediate, arbitrate, and/or to listen carefully. All of these skills require different approaches, which can be non-verbal or spoken. Using and practising the 'discussion steps' below are important life skills, as well as being useful for working through emerging issues.

However, the conclusions of a piece of research conducted between 1996 and 2004 by Kingston Friends Workshop Group (KFWG) entitled *Preventing and Responding to Bullying* found that for any lasting change to take place in establishing collaborative multi-agency working, there needs to be some recognition and support by those in authority for concerns raised by practitioners, children, and families. The support can come from a variety of sources, including a room used for meetings, an open-door policy for parents and carers, and attendance by setting governors at specific events. In other words, for any long-term effects to be seen, heard, and felt, it is important to have working collaborations and an environment that recognizes and values all contributions from all the agencies locally and nationally. Any change relies on using the energy created by conflict, knowledge, theory, and practice. It is not the conflict, problem or issue that matters, but how we use knowledge, theory, and practice to respond creatively that pushes the boundaries and moves things forward.

Observing a concern/issue/conflict/debate

Come to an agreement with a colleague to make a conscious decision to watch either a television programme that has a conflict (soaps are useful!) or listen to a radio/television programme that has some kind of educational issue, conflict or debate that needs resolving and make some notes. Practise taking notes in the style that suits you, as detailed in Chapter 3. Use the following framework to have a discussion with a fellow practitioner and compare your findings.

Discussion steps

1. Write down the key points of the issue as you heard discussed.
2. List what the feelings were around the issues by those discussing it.
3. Who suggested any ways of resolving the issue?
4. What was the final outcome?
5. Was it satisfactory in your view?
6. Can you think of any other ways the issue could have been resolved?

These simple steps are extremely useful in any context and can be used to explore a shared concern. They can also be used to explore assignment criteria, a curriculum issue, ways of working, how to collect evidence, or to find out how to establish a baseline for a piece of work-based learning. Just as different disciplines and agencies use their own interpretations, language, and traditions, so does research. The six steps above are adapted from the mediation framework and have been presented in different guises by a variety of research disciplines. However, the steps used in other disciplines do not normally include feelings, yet these can be a driving force in either creating barriers or removing them.

Having become familiar with the Key Components Framework, practised a focused discussion using a variety of hidden skills, and identified different language skills for debate, use the following activity with a group of practitioners to experience, in a friendly non-threatening environment, a multi-disciplinary problem that needs to be resolved. Choose one person as an observer and that person is to use the 'discussion steps' above to provide feedback at the end of the debate.

The importance of multi-agency working is not new but the emphasis on the role of the other statutory agencies in taking responsibility is changing due in part to the new Childcare Act 2006. This change in emphasis is clearly supported not only by the government's Green Paper, *Every Child Matters* (2003). but also by the Laming Enquiry Recommendations (2003):

> The Department of Health must establish a common language for use across *all agencies* to help those agencies to identify, who they are concerned about, why they are concerned, who is best placed to respond to those concerns and what outcome is being sought from any planned response.
>
> (Laming Enquiry Recommendations 2003: 373)

The following activity explores responses to a family situation by a multi-agency group of people and provides a focus for decision making.

Multi-professional workshop group activity

Group activity for six participants and one observer

Resource pack containing:

- six envelopes, each with information about Bradley and the experience of ONE key person – early years practitioner, senior coordinator, manager/head teacher, parent, social worker, health visitor;
- pre-assessment checklist (can be downloaded from the internet);
- Common Assessment Framework (CAF) form (can be downloaded from the internet);

- guide to definitions used in a CAF form (can be downloaded from the internet);
- strips of coloured paper to make a simple headband or a label with the named role for each professional;
- scissors, labels, stapler, and felt pen.

Objectives:

- to work as a team, with each individual actively participating in role;
- to hold a multi-professional meeting to address Bradley's current identified needs.
- to complete a CAF form for Bradley if needed;
- out of role – to reflect and evaluate on the learning process.

Group task

You have all been invited by the setting senior coordinator to a meeting in response to an initial concern about Bradley voiced by his early years practitioner. Normally, the early years practitioner/senior coordinator would already have completed a pre-assessment sheet, having met informally with Bradley's parents and agreed with them to seek further support.

1. Take one envelope each, read the two sheets and create a headband or label for yourself in role.
2. Choose a chair/leader for the meeting. The person who has called the meeting may choose to act as chair.
3. Set up the meeting.
4. Use the CAF form to focus your discussion, completing relevant boxes as you proceed. The chair or one other may act as scribe.
5. Close the meeting.
6. Reflect as a group on your learning experience.

Background

Bradley is the younger of two children. He is four years old. His sister is seven. They live with their alcoholic mother who is currently receiving support from her general practitioner to stop drinking. She has been attending regular meetings and making 'good progress'. The children do not have contact with their father who left when Bradley was born. The family lives in council accommodation on a large housing estate. They are currently housed in a two-bedroom flat. They are known to Social Services and the Police Service, as there has been a history of domestic violence and public order offences. The family has no living relatives, but a neighbour often brings the children to school. Bradley is in the nursery and his sister is in Year 2.

Roles

You are the early years practitioner:

- You are becoming increasingly concerned as to the physical condition of Bradley. He regularly attends school dirty and hungry. He has a severe case of headlice and you suspect that he has impetigo on his face. The other children have noticed that he smells, which is affecting his self-esteem. You have spoken to his mother on two occasions and she has made promises of better care. She assures the staff that the doctor diagnosed the rash on his face as eczema.
- You have informed the senior coordinator.
- You have made contact with Bradley's sister's class teacher who is also experiencing similar concerns.
- The senior coordinator has requested a meeting with the mother, Social Services, and the school to discuss the situation.

You want assurances that Bradley and his sister will receive appropriate care and feel emotionally involved in the situation as you have suspicions that their mother is drinking heavily again and may be incapable of looking after them.

You are the head teacher:

- You are concerned with the physical condition of the child.
- You have heard that the mother is drinking heavily and are anxious for the safety of the children.
- You are also concerned that staff members are increasingly involving themselves in washing, feeding, and clothing the child. You are aware of the possible ramifications of this in terms of allegations that could be made.

You are anxious to find a resolution without antagonizing the mother and causing allegations against staff members who have washed and changed the child on a number of occasions.

You are the senior coordinator:

- You are aware of a history of domestic abuse in the family. You are also aware that the mother is an alcoholic and have heard 'on the grapevine' that she is drinking heavily again.

- You feel that the children are not being cared for and are suffering from neglect.
- You are concerned for the children's welfare and safety.

You are keen for Social Services to remove the children from danger and house them in temporary accommodation until matters are resolved.

You are a member of the Social Services team that has been working with the family over a number of years:

- You appreciate the circumstances that have preceded this meeting and understand that the mother has been under extreme pressure recently as the father of the children has moved close by.
- The history of domestic abuse has been reignited in the mother's view and she is frightened, although there have been no further incidents. There has been a relapse in her drinking programme of recovery, although she has requested further help. There is a possibility that the mother might have to go to court to stop the father of the children harassing them.
- The mother has requested that this information is not shared at this meeting.

You are keen for the children to remain with their mother as you feel it would not be in their interests to move at present.

You are Bradley's mother:

- You suffered domestic abuse at the hands of your ex-partner, the father of your children.
- Over time, you became an alcoholic.
- Your ex-partner left you when you had Bradley.
- With Social Services support you have been re-housed and have been able to get help via your general practitioner for your drinking habit. You have made very good progress and the children have been cared for.
- You live for your children and will not let anyone interfere with their upbringing.
- The recent shock of your ex-partner moving close by has caused upset. Although he is unaware of where you live, you are frightened. The prospect of him living nearby has caused a relapse in your drinking programme. However, you have maintained contact with Social Services and they have been very supportive. They are currently trying to find alternative accommodation for you and the children.

You are very angry with the school:

- While you appreciate that your mind has been 'a bit mixed up' lately, you will not have them interfere with your life. You do not want them knowing your business.
- You do not have anyone but your elderly neighbour to help you with the children and you get very tired of trying to cope on a limited budget.
- The children have free school packed lunches, so the school should know that they are fed.

You want the school to leave you alone.

You are the health visitor attached to the family's general practitioner and have known the family since Bradley was born:

- You have been aware of a history of domestic abuse in the family. You have had no recent information about changes in the family pattern. You are also aware that the mother is an alcoholic and suspected, on a home visit to the family, that she is drinking again. You told the general practitioner about your concern and he has helped you encourage her to attend a small group at the health centre. You know she is going regularly, as a colleague runs the group.
- You also know she is determined to bring up the children well and lives for them. You have become increasingly concerned that her level of care for the children is not the same now they are growing up. She seems to expect them to take more responsibility for themselves – washing, dressing, and preparing food. You have tried to share knowledge about their abilities and child development but are unsure if you have been heard.
- Bradley and his sister always welcome you when you visit, so you have decided to go monthly at present to keep in touch. You are about to complete Bradley's health records for his first five years and will need to confirm whether you maintain contact with the family.

This activity works well if it can be used with a group of practitioners from a variety of disciplines. What are the outcomes and how were decisions made? Who took the lead? Did any boundary issues emerge?

References

Children's Workforce Development Council (2007) www.cwdccouncil.org.uk/integratedworking (*(accessed September 2007)*. London: CWDC.

Department for Education and Skills (2005) Common Core of Skills and Knowledge for the Children's Workforce. London: DfES.

Department for Education and Skills (2003) *Green Paper: Every Child Matters.* London: DfES.

Department for Education and Skills (2004a) *Every Child Matters: Change for Children.* London: DfES.

Department for Education and Skills (2004b) *Strategy for Childcare.* London: DfES.

Department for Education and Skills (2004c) *The Children Act.* London: DfES.

Department for Education and Skills (2004d) *Choice for Parents, the Best Start for Children: A Ten Year Strategy for Childcare.* London: HMSO.

Department for Education and Skills (2006a) *Implementing the Disability Discrimination Act in Schools and Early Years Settings.* London: DfES.

Department for Education and Skills (2006b) *The Childcare Act.* London: DfES

Improvement and Development Agency (1995)

Kingston Friends Workshop Group (1996) *Preventing and Responding to Bullying.* Kingston: KFWG.

Miller, C., Freeman, M. and Ross, N. (2001) *Interprofessional Practice in Health and Social Care: Challenging the Learning Agenda.* London: Arnold.

SureStart (2006) www.surestart.gov.uk/aboutsurestart/about/strategy (accessed 22 July 2008). London: SureStart.

PART 2
PRACTICE

6 Contemporary issues in relation to early years theory and practice

All children are artists. The problem is
how to remain an artist once s/he
grows up.

Pablo Picasso

This chapter outlines areas that relate to early years theory and practice and
discusses concerns that are affecting current practitioners in their settings.
Having reviewed assignment titles on all the early years courses, from foundation degrees, BA (Hons), and initial teacher training to the MA for the past
two years, it would appear that the areas uppermost in practitioners' concerns
cover the following:

- outdoor learning;
- transition from Foundation Stage to Key Stage 1;
- transition from home to school;
- transition to new Early Years Foundation Stage (birth to five years);
- child development (birth to three years);
- aspects of play;
- working with families;
- speech and language difficulties;
- creativity;
- inclusion;
- instigating a 'Reggio Emilia' approach to teaching and learning;
- special educational needs;
- new roles and responsibilities;
- English as an additional language;
- information and communication technologies across the
  curriculum;
- behaviour;
- developing early years units;
- autism;
- child development in terms of delay/difficulty.

Further down the list are:

- assessment;
- time for planning, preparation, and assessment;
- diversity and equal opportunities;
- mathematics;
- phonics.

Acknowledging and considering children's culture today

Defining children's culture would make a book on its own and there are many ways to define the concept of culture. The very core of culture is about reflecting on something that we are all part of today and yet it is also about our own yesterdays. For example, although I grew up in Yorkshire and the north-east, as an adult I have lived in London for the past 35 years. However, I still feel I am 'going home' whenever I go to the north-east (Key Components Framework Strand 2). Our view of 'culture' will always be in some way limited by our experience and understanding. We will all be affected by what surrounds us on a day-to-day basis but also affected by our yesterdays.

National and international perspectives can also impact on teaching and learning. For example, the Reggio Emilia approach to learning is currently being adapted and used in many settings (KCF Strands 1 and 3). Culture today is complex, dynamic, and can be influenced by a variety of events, natural phenomena, other cultures, and outside influences.

An important aspect of children's culture is that they do not have the 'freedom' that adults have to make changes in their lives so easily, particularly if they are not in a 'good' or 'safe' place. *Every Child Matters* (DfES 2003) is one of the driving forces to safeguarding vulnerable children. The appointment of a Children's Commissioner in the UK is a step towards giving children a voice. The Children's Society (http://www.childrenssociety.org.uk/) 'provides help and understanding for those forgotten children who are unable to find the support they need anywhere else' (accessed 26 November 2007). The current Schools Minister, Andrew Adonis (17 November 2007), said:

> Improving the life chances of children with special educational needs and disabilities is an absolute priority for us. A key part of that is equipping teachers with the skills and confidence to help children with a range of special educational needs. We have the best trained workforce ever and many teachers are already offering children with SEN [special educational needs] high levels of teaching and support. This new training, developed in partnership with I CAN and Dyslexia Action, builds on this by offering teachers every day opportunities to

continue developing their skills in the classroom so that all children with special needs can access the help they need. The training materials will initially focus on speech, language and communication needs and dyslexia. Over the next four years training on autistic spectrum disorders, behavioural issues and moderate learning difficulties will be added.

Article 23 of the United Nations Convention on the Rights of the Child (1989) states that, 'A disabled child has the right to special care, education and training to help him or her enjoy a full and decent life in dignity and achieve the greatest degree of self reliance and social integration possible.'

Some may say that taking a very young child, particularly a disabled child, and putting him or her in a setting with lots of other children for most of the day could be harmful. There are several recent pieces of research that indicate that the *quality of care* received is key to young babies (up to 36 months) feeling stressed or not in a daycare setting.

> Our main finding was that at daycare children display higher cortisol levels compared to the home setting. Diurnal patterns revealed significant increases from morning to afternoon, but at daycare only. We examined all papers on possible associations between cortisol levels and quality of care, and the influences of age, gender, and children's temperament. Age appeared to be the most significant moderator of this relation. It was shown that the effect of daycare attendance on cortisol excretion was especially notable in children younger than 36 months. We speculate that children in daycare show elevated cortisol levels because of their stressful interactions in a group setting.
>
> (Vermeer and van Ijzendoorn 2006: 390–91)

As children's learning environments are at the heart of what practitioners are working hard to improve, it is natural to explore the culture of their lives to hear and respond to their needs. Any assignment should have regard to their voice from a variety of perspectives. Family life today is very different to the one I grew up in. I still remember with fondness 'Listen with Mother' with Andy Pandy and friends and although they acted out a variety of issues to do with friendship, caring for others, and being tidy, they were put away in a box at the end of each programme and brought out again the next time the programme opened. It was not what was on the television, although this was a novelty in itself, so much as my mother sitting with me for a short space of time and enjoying the programme with me. I was not left on my own with the television on. I do not remember having any toys associated with the programmes apart from Muffin the Mule, which I still own. Most of the stories were about being kind, finding ways of solving problems or making friends.

Dan Fleming (1996: 4), who has written extensively on children's toys, comments that:

> Giant toy makers often do research with children to try and discover what will be the next big seller. In the early eighties they asked girls what they saw when they closed their eyes. Time and time again they got the answer – horses – it led to 200 million plastic horses with brushable manes being sold – 'my little pony' videos and comics relating to the ponies tell stories of affection and domestic conviviality.

Many children wanted a Buzz Light Year after seeing the film of *Toy Story* and more recently *Wallace and Gromit* and *Monsters Inc*. In America, dolls are big business with a whole experience built around them, including a day out designing a doll to a child's specification with a matching outfit for the owner of the doll, a hairstyle of the doll owner's choice, and a meal and photograph taken with the newly named doll. This also raises issues relating to gender bias but as it appears to be enjoyed by so many girls, who are adults not to listen to their voice? In the main, however, it is adults guiding these activities. If left to their own devices, what would children choose to do?

In a letter to the *Daily Telegraph* (12/09/08), 110 teachers, psychologists, children's authors, and other experts called on the government to act to prevent the death of childhood. They wrote:

> We are deeply concerned at the escalating incidence of childhood depression and children's behavioural and developmental conditions. The group, which includes Philip Pullman, the children's author, Jacqueline Wilson, the children's laureate, her predecessor Michael Morpurgo, Baroness Greenfield, the director of the Royal Institution and Dr Penelope Leach, the child care expert, blames a failure by politicians and public alike to understand how children develop. Since children's brains are still developing, they cannot adjust . . . to the effects of ever more rapid technological and cultural change.

Today's toys are often linked to texts and visual images. Big books and narrative texts are sometimes made into films, DVDs, and CD-Roms. Today's children live in a very visual and multi-sensory world and most have either a television, often in their bedrooms, or gaming console even from a young age. The Literacy Trust website recently reported a study from America of the effects of television. Rideout *et al.* (2005) found a link between television viewing and reading: 'In heavy TV households (where the TV is switched on most of the time), 24 per cent of children aged two and over could read; in other homes the figure was 36 per cent.' The survey also found that a quarter of American children under two have a TV in their bedroom. However, the researchers did not find a gender divide at these young ages. They also found that boys and girls begin to use computers at around two years of age. There were, however, issues relating to weight gain, with children who watched more television being heavier than those who watched for less than two hours.

Children's futures and how we develop teaching and learning strategies in the new framework (birth to age five) depend on a much deeper understanding of children's culture, developmental factors, and current knowledge of research that affects how children develop and learn. The Primary National Strategy (DfES 2007a) suggests that:

> families at the start of the new millennium are different from fifty years ago, but as Jagger and Wright (1999: p. 3) point out, 'the family is neither a pan-human universal nor a stable or essential entity . . . Families and relations are, like the term itself, flexible, fluid and contingent'. Therefore, at a time when families are fragmented and isolated for many different reasons, we need to explore ways of ensuring that all babies and young children feel part of a family, however that is constituted.

Transition from the home to a setting for a young child can be an emotional event for both the parents/carers and the child. The early-years sector is complex and there are many different types of settings, from childminders, toddler groups, playgroups, and daycare through to nursery.

> Such is the significance of early transitions for young children that it is essential that parents/carers, educators, policy makers and politicians pay close attention to children's early experiences in order to provide well for them.
>
> (Fabian and Dunlop 2002: 2)

In turn, this requires practitioners to be creative, reflective thinkers who can respond appropriately to an individual child's needs, particularly the learning environment they provide for them.

Cultural considerations for a play-based environment

The Early Years Foundation Stage (DfES 2007b) states that:

> Children's play reflects their wide ranging and varied interests and preoccupations. In their play children learn at their highest level. Play with peers is important for children's development.
>
> (4.1 Play and Exploration)

Most early years practitioners value and see the importance of play. However, some believe that play has somehow become marginalized by outside factors, in particular practitioners working with four- to five-year-olds in a reception class. Comments I have heard include the following:

> 'After we have done the literacy and numeracy there is not much time left for play'. (Reception class)
> *What are the underlying assumptions?*
>
> 'What about resources, space and staffing for all that outdoor play?'(Practitioner)
> *What are the underlying assumptions?*
>
> 'I am paying a lot of money to send my child here. I want my children to learn.' (Parent)
> *What are the underlying assumptions?*
>
> 'I have given up my job so I can play with my child at home. I want you to teach my child.' (Parent – Daycare)
> *What are the underlying assumptions?*
>
> 'Parents think the children are playing all day and really just want the children to learn to read and write.' (Practitioner)
> *What are the underlying assumptions?*
>
> 'I will have difficulty in my setting introducing a play-based curriculum because the Key Stage 1 Standard Assessment Tests (SATs) results were high and staff will fear a drop in standards.' (Deputy head teacher setting up an early years unit)
> *What are the underlying assumptions?*

It is interesting to note that the National Curriculum (DfES 2006) stresses the importance of play in the development of thinking skills but it is not mentioned in the communication part of the document.

The interrelationships that occur between children, families, and the learning community depend on all the people that attend a setting. Values and beliefs will vary, which is why it is important to include everyone when refining or developing a policy including the children (see Chapter 4 for further explanation). The introduction of the new Early Years Foundation Stage (DfES 2007b) will provide opportunities for those who would like to explore and change/improve the play-based curriculum in their setting. There appears to be mixed views on play from parents and carers. Some parents and carers value learning through play and some are more sceptical.

Themes that commonly occur throughout the world can be built upon with all children, such as eating, sleeping, drinking, and becoming ill. What makes them culturally different is that which is eaten and drunk, types of illness, and how they sleep. For practitioners this requires a secure knowledge base of other cultures and a commitment to sharing one's own beliefs and values. It also requires an in-depth knowledge of how children play and the ability to observe play behaviour to reliably track and evaluate children's progress. Many theorists have defined play behaviours (Piaget 1962; Bruner 1966; Bruce 1997); however, to observe, track, and evaluate learning through play, it can be said that it is 'observable, describable, and repeatable' in different contexts. How this relates to theory in practice depends on deeper learning through in-depth reading, ongoing monitoring, and experience.

From birth, children develop preferences for interactions with people and objects. In a research report, Stephen *et al.* (2003) highlighted the following:

> 3–12 month infants gain increasing pleasure from vocal play and song, and the emphasis on expressive play required from caregivers (not largely reliant on toys or other material resources) fosters the child's disposition to learn in company. At 9–24 months a growing vocabulary comes along with a repertoire of gestures, behaviours and imitations.

The authors also highlight that practitioners are the most important resource in out-of-home provision.

Dispositions

There is much brain research on different literacies and the effects into children's 'literacies' development. One of these literacies is visual. Visual literacy is enhanced by using multi-sensory experiences, which is advocated in the Early Years Foundation Stage documents (Creative Development 3, 5, and 6). Many other 'literacies' depend on visual and sensory input, including speaking and listening for communication. Courses such as enhancing communication between babies and adults through the use of signing are on the increase.

Ros Bayley is well known for her work on the differences between the way that boys and girls develop. In a recent article on the differences between boys' and girls' brain development and whether boys are more disadvantaged than girls in early years settings, she states that in some cases:

> Boys and girls are different. Their bodies and brains develop differently and at different rates and not to take account of this when we work is madness! Their physical and educational needs are different and to try to make them the same will not work. However, by approximately eight or nine years of age children can lose up to half of the neurons that their brain uses to 'make connections' to other parts of the brain.
>
> (Bayley 2007: 37–42)

Therefore, the time between birth and 8 years of age is crucial in establishing these connections.

The Early Years Foundation Stage (DfES 2007b) breaks down each area of learning into different aspects. Personal, social, and emotional learning, for example, are broken down as follows:

- disposition and attitudes;
- self-confidence and self-esteem;
- making relationships;
- behaviour and self-control;
- self-care;
- sense of community.

A child's disposition and attitude to learning can depend on personality, cognitive ability, environments (indoor/outdoor), relationships, events, and motivation. According to Sharon Airey (2005: 225): 'Children are not born with attitudes; they form them as a result of exposure to their family, parents, experiences, local/wider society, media, peers, practitioners, teachers and carers.' The cultural context a young child grows up in may embrace individualism, where dispositions leading to self-enhancement are encouraged, or collectivism, promoting dispositions of sharing and empathizing with others.

In their ongoing studies of how young children socialize, Howes and James (2002) are aware of the need to identify influential key factors within non-parental childcare. The framework below 'incorporates key dimensions for understanding processes of socialization within childcare'.

The first assumption made in this model (Figure 6.1) is that the relationship history and dispositions a child brings into childcare are consistent or inconsistent with 'positive social interactions and relationships'. The second assumption is that both dispositions and relationship history will contribute to the construction of positive child–caregiver relationships and to positive peer-group interactions and relationships. 'If children have these dispositions or are helped to develop them within childcare they are more likely to engage in harmonious interactions with others and to develop positive relationships with others' (Howes and Richie, cited in Howes and James 2002: 148).

A closer look at 'disposition and attitudes' can reveal hidden assumptions and cultural values. This has to be considered alongside the internal working model of adult–child attachments and values and beliefs that the child, new into childcare, brings from family and previous childcare experiences. Also, the implication is that dispositions can be developed, rather than the child just having to cope with the biological given. There are implications here for the practitioner in early years, since it is well-documented that 'children with positive child–caregiver relationships appear more able to make use of the learning opportunities available in childcare and construct more positive peer relationships in childcare and as older children' (Carr 2001, cited in Lindon 2005: 105).

Howes and James (2002) make a plea for all the dimensions in this model to be addressed in future studies on socialization within childcare. There is scope for practitioners to add to the knowledge base of the impact of dispositions – whether innate or nurtured – on social development.

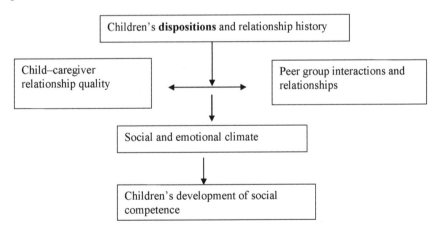

Figure 6.1 A model for understanding processes of socialization within childcare.

Lillian Katz (cited in Lindon 2005: 104) saw dispositions as 'habits of mind and a pattern of behaviour that is directed to a broad goal'. This implies that they can be formed within and by social context, allowing adults and the surrounding environment to influence the dispositions of children.

Dispositions include knowledge, skills, and attitudes. Te Whriki, the New Zealand curriculum for early years, acknowledges positive dispositions, meaning 'an outlook, attitudes and pattern of behaviour that will support children to be, and to want to be, learners'.

The five key areas of learning dispositions identified by Margaret Carr (2001: p17) and included in the above are as follows:

- taking an interest;
- being involved;
- communicating with others;
- taking responsibility;
- persisting with difficulty or uncertainty.

Practitioners are bound to identify with the impact of these in daily practice. Carr broke up each area into three parts for closer consideration: (1) being ready, (2) being willing, and (3) being able. The Early Years Foundation Stage (DfES 2007b) draws on these studies. Informed practitioners can influence the development of dispositions for learning and this area certainly provides scope for practitioner research.

Research has also linked play to cognitive, social, linguistic, and emotional development. The idea of the child as a re-constructor is indispensable. We all know of children that will make a ship out of a box and suddenly it will be a spaceship or a twig that becomes a gun. 'In their play children learn at their highest level' (DfES 2007b). Interpreting play behaviours requires rigorous observations to collect compelling evidence about children's learning.

List how you would collect compelling evidence that demonstrates the following environment for teaching and learning through play.
The collection of evidence also needs to take into consideration whether the setting environment is responsive to the following:

- the spontaneous needs of children playing;
- the environment facilitating children choosing their own materials for activities;
- adult-/child-led resources;
- how committed staff members are to a child-led play based environment;
- whether planning responds to the needs and interests of the children or whether everything is pre-planned;
- how the organization of the day needs to be adjusted.

The EYFS [Early Years Foundation Stage] is based on principles of inclusion which means that early years providers oppose

> discrimination and prejudice and welcome all families and children. They provide care and education for a wide range of children in environments that enable children to feel safe and supported and which extend their learning and development.
>
> (DfES 2007b)

The government's Green Paper, *Excellence for all Children: Meeting Special Educational Needs* (HMSO 1997), focuses on early intervention and pre-ventative work. It envisaged that health, education, and social care are organized around children and their families promoting a coordinated approach. The development of children's centres, extended schools, and children's trusts has been to increase the availability of appropriate care for children and young people.

For the practitioner, there are many opportunities to begin to explore what looks on the page as a simple concept, but in reality is loaded with assumptions, values, and beliefs. It is important for the practitioner to understand that embarking on a work-based project is really the start of a continuum of learning cycles. According to Cowne (2003: 32), there are some 'golden rules' the work-based practitioner research needs to follow:

- small is beautiful – choose a manageable task;
- go with the flow – choose an aspect of on-going work;
- don't get eaten for breakfast! – work with the positive side of the system.

Because work-based practitioner research proceeds in cycles, the cycles can be repeated over and over again or stopped at any time. This is useful, as it enables reflection and evaluation in more detail. Ideally, the cycles can continue over a long period of time to see a pattern emerging or they can be small and only appertain to one area.

References

Airey, S. (2004) Inclusive practice in early years, in T. Maynard and N. Thomas (eds) *An Introduction to Early Childhood Studies*. London: Sage.

Bayley, R. (2007) Gender issues in early education, *EYE Focus Magazine*, 8(9): 37–42.

Bruce, T. (1997) *Early Childhood Education* (2nd revised edn.). London: Hodder Arnold.

Bruner, J. (1966) *Towards a Theory of Instruction*. Cambridge, MA: Belknap Press.

Carr, M. (2001) *Assessment in Early Childhood Settings*. London: Paul Chapman.

Cowne, E. (2003) *Developing Inclusive Practice: The SENCO's Role in Managing Change*. London: David Fulton Publishers.

Daily Telegraph 12, September 2008.

Department for Children, Schools and Families (2007) *Boost for Children with Special Educational Needs* (retrieved 17 November 2007 from: www.dcsf.org.uk).

Department for Education and Skills (2003) *Green Paper: Every Child Matters.* London: DfES.

Department for Education and Skills (2006) *The National Curriculum.* London: DfES.

Department for Education and Skills (2007a) *The Primary National Strategy.* London: DfES.

Department for Education and Skills (2007b) *Early Years Foundation Stage: Setting the Standards for Learning, Development and Care from Birth to Five.* London: DfES.

Fabian, D. and Dunlop, W. (2002) *Transitions in the Early Years: Debating Continuity and Progression for Children in Early Years Education.* Oxford: Blackwell Publishers.

Fleming, S. (1996) *Powerplay: Toys as Popular Culture.* Manchester: Manchester University Press.

HMSO (1997) *Green Paper. Excellence for all Children: Meeting Special Educational Needs.* London: The Stationery Office.

Howes, C. and James, J. (2002) *Children's Social Development.* Oxford: Blackwell.

Lindon, J. (2005) *Understanding Child Development: Linking Theory and Practice.* London: Hodder Arnold.

Piaget, J. (1962) *Play, Dreams and Imitation in Childhood.* New York: W.W. Norton.

Rideout, V., Vandewater, E.A. and Wartella, E.A. (2003) *Zero to Six: Electronic Media Use in the Lives of Infants, Toddlers and Preschoolers.* Menlo Park, CA: Kaiser Family Foundation.

Stephen, C., Dunlop, A.-W. and Trevarthen, C. (2003) *Meeting the Needs of Children from Birth to Three: Research Evidence and Implications for Out-of-home Provision.* Edinburgh: The Scottish Executive.

UNICEF (1989) *The United Nations Convention on the Rights of the Child.* New York: UNICEF.

Vermeer, H.J. and van Ijzendoorn, M.H. (2006) Children's elevated cortisol levels at daycare: a review and meta-analysis, *Early Childhood Research Quarterly*, 21(3): 390–401.

7 Work-based practitioner: learning to research

The mark of a good action is that it appears inevitable in retrospect.

Robert Louis Stevenson

Practitioner research methodology

Evidence from Kingston University's work-based learners supports the fact that shared learning can and does influence practice. Being able to self-reflect is a keystone for any practitioner.

> The idea of self-reflection is central. In traditional forms of research – empirical research – researchers do research on other people. In action research, researchers do research on themselves. Empirical researchers enquire into other people's lives. Action researchers enquire into their own lives. Action research is an enquiry conducted by the self into the self. You, a practitioner, think about your own life and work, and this involves you asking yourself why you do the things that you do, and why you are the way that you are. When you produce your research report, it shows how you have carried out a systematic investigation into your own behaviour, and the reasons for that behaviour. The report shows the process you have gone through in order to achieve a better understanding of yourself, so that you can continue developing yourself and your work.
>
> (McNiff and Whitehead 2005: 46–49)

Terminology in relation to any kind of research is dependent upon the type being carried out and a person's personal perspective. It is all too easy to become frustrated and overwhelmed with the discourse on terminology about research that it becomes what Anderson (cited in Haywood Metz and Page 2005: 26–27) calls a 'murky swamp'. It is important to examine practice from several perspectives. Let us return to the Key Components Framework, grow model, and discussion steps to remain focused on why, what, where, and how to investigate practice.

In a work-based learning environment, you are striving to provide explanations, reasons, and evidence as to why you make the decisions that affect your learning and children's learning. This is not just for the course, but part of a personal philosophy that reaches the heart of any improvements for the future (KCF Strands 2 and 3). The previous chapters have looked at setting a personal and professional baseline and ask you to take stock of your current theory, knowledge, skills, and understanding, and the impact on your learning. Some courses, including those at Kingston, ask that you keep a portfolio of this learning over a period of time. Any change to improve personal practice involves risk taking. This can be challenging, especially when it includes others in the workplace as well as being open to scrutiny by tutors. However, a well-planned assignment involving learning at work can be very rewarding. It starts by asking questions, which can be categorized in many ways. The following are some initial questions based on the discussion questions in Chapter 4:

1. Which area of my practice am I really interested in and would like to develop?
2. Why am I interested in this area?
3. What are my concerns, issues?
4. What do I feel about it?
5. What is the main content of my investigation?
6. How am I going to set up my investigation?
7. What and how am I going to collect evidence?
8. How will I judge if I have been successful?

The last question is probably the most difficult to answer in early years, as much of what work-based practitioners do may only be realized in the long term.

Creating possibilities is exciting, as this is a chance to make a difference. It can be difficult in the first instance to decide on what area of practice to change or improve and this can appear to be a negative approach. However, unless there is an acknowledgement that there is always room for further learning and improvement, it is back to the 'wasteland'! In previous chapters, we have considered the following:

- theory;
- early years context;
- definitions – roles and responsibilities;
- different disciplines – their language and codes;
- pedagogy – type of learners and ways of teaching;

- curriculum – transition towards the new Early Years Foundation Stage (Statutory 2008);
- policy relating to practice;
- ethical considerations.

Having identified an area you are interested in, the next step is to transform that area into a specific question. Remember, 'small is beautiful' when setting out to do any kind of practitioner research. Make sure that you have looked at both the generic and specific criteria for any assignment before you start. The generic criteria relate to the specified grading and its guidelines that each university has to ensure parity with other universities. In other words, it is used to mark work in line with that of other students at the level you are now working. Each university has external examiners from other universities that look across work, often from several universities.

Specific criteria are used to ensure that students have guidelines that relate to a particular assignment. It will be in a curriculum, pedagogic, theoretical or social policy area. You will need to demonstrate in your assignment the ability to engage with theoretical reading, critically evaluate your learning and making informed decisions with the intention of improving the quality of learning experiences for children. The children must be at the heart of the quest to improve practice.

The following are questions you might ask yourself depending on the type of improvement you would like to make.

Question categories

Reflective questions

Examples:

How can I . . .

    initiate
    promote through . . .
    develop . . .
    extend and . . .
    enhance . . .
    monitor . . .
    track . . .
    evaluate . . .
    share . . .
    challenge and . . .
    produce . . .

link . . .
judge if I . . .
measure . . .
embed . . .

Sometimes you can put two of these aspects together. It may be that you would like to investigate an area that has not been so successful for a variety of reasons, in which case you may be looking for a causal link between them.

Causal and relationship questions

Example:

Does . . . support/enhance/ . . . or would it . . .?
Why do patterns of . . . between . . . and . . .?
What are the factors that would enhance . . . and how can I . . .?
Would a group of six circle time workshops . . . improve . . .?

Descriptive questions usually begin with what, why, how or where.
Here are some questions that have been used for assignments. Look critically at them and decide if they are appropriate for researching. List your reasons for each of the answers:

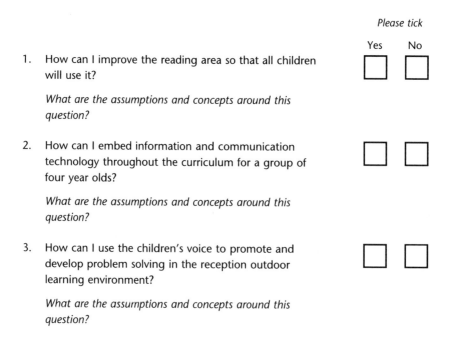

Please tick

Yes No

1. How can I improve the reading area so that all children will use it?

    What are the assumptions and concepts around this question?

2. How can I embed information and communication technology throughout the curriculum for a group of four year olds?

    What are the assumptions and concepts around this question?

3. How can I use the children's voice to promote and develop problem solving in the reception outdoor learning environment?

    What are the assumptions and concepts around this question?

4. How can I improve the transition process between the
    Foundation Stage and Key Stage 1 to help to ensure the
    provision of an environment that supports continuity
    and progression in learning?

    *What are the assumptions and concepts around this
    question?*

5. How can I build on the children's current interests in
    mini-beasts to extend cross-curricular learning?

    *What are the assumptions and concepts around this
    question?*

Once you have decided on a working title, make time to read around the
area. Be careful to include reading that looks at the boundaries if doing an
extended piece of work that is multi-professional in nature. You may need to
access books on health and social care as well as education for this aspect.
What might be the constraints to setting up a small piece of practitioner
research or extended study?

Collecting evidence: what am I going to collect and how am I going to collect it?

The key question is now identified and background reading is under way. This
is the time more questions are likely to arise, which links the knowledge being
gained and work-based practice. The reflective log can be a place to record
these issues so that they do not interfere with the original focus, or if they
persist, work with them so that they become part of the research. Look for
direct links between theory and practice that will help in both the choice of
specific evidence and later critical analysis.

The strength of practitioner research is that you are open to the daily
opportunities within your grasp to improve early years care and education
through the knowledge, skills, and abilities of those around you – staff, parents, and children – and the environment that you are living in – your 'real
world' (Robson 1993: 2). It is at this point that many practitioners flinch at
the need to include others, for example:

- other staff are already so busy they will have no time for me;
- the parents have to drop off/collect their children quickly, so there is
  no time to meet with them;
- we have to leave the premises in a certain way when we finish, so I
  really cannot allow the 'process' of this project to continue for days.

Work-based practitioner learners develop courage and increased confidence during their studies. These are situations to identify honestly and work *with* rather than cover up. It is hard when some of the peer group are working in settings that encourage and facilitate them to try out so much more than others. Yet, in a true learning community, they too will learn that an additional strength of practitioner research is to value differences within practice and look for ways to support each other with these challenges. This enriches professional practice within a wider learning community. These practicalities are realistically best faced *before* choosing what evidence to collect and how to collect it. Differentiate the 'time' factors within demanding circumstances from the anxiety of having to relate to others, and address each separately. The first requires realistic organizational skills, the second assertive communication and cooperative skills.

The choice of what to collect naturally depends on the question or topic. Within work-based study, there is a range of key topics to be explored, including:

- learning and development – for babies, children, and adults;
- developing and sustaining parent partnerships;
- personalized learning;
- ownership of 'sustained, share thinking';
- multi-professional/multi-agency working;
- monitoring, assessment, and planning;
- staff development;
- transitions;
- outdoor learning;
- introducing and embedding new government initiatives;
- leadership and management skills;
- child-initiated and adult-initiated activities.

This list is not definitive but indicates areas of current concern for many.

Evidence has to show what has happened. Are work-based learners more likely to seek quantitative evidence or qualitative evidence, or a mixture of the two? *Quantitative evidence* provides data, often statistical, that will provide a general statement for others to replicate. The researcher tries to be objective throughout so that the validity of the result will be through others implementing the same procedures with the same outcome. This is the positivist, scientific research tradition.

A hypothesis/question is set to discover the 'truth' about a key issue, such as: 'Is there a difference in word-recognition ability between boys and girls at the age of four?' Proving this would require large samples of 'experiments' and observations/tests in controlled conditions working to specific criteria.

How specific can you be in the workplace when working with individuals or groups of babies and children?

Interpretive research has developed within the social sciences as a result of the emphasis on interaction within social contexts. Roberts-Holmes (2005: 39) likens this to 'close-up detailed photographs. These show the fine detail and complex interactions going on'. This *qualitative research* lends itself to use in the variety of early years care and education contexts, but leads the researcher to face up to the inevitable subjectivity and potential bias in their work. Peter Elfer (2005: 120) introduces an adaptation of the 'Tavistock Method' of observation as a way to help the early years practitioner researcher reflect on the emotional as well as the sensory effects arising from the experience. This will be discussed in more detail later. The process is seen as key evidence and so requires time and effort in using tools to justify the events as they occur within the workplace. How do you document the energy and vitality of young children and the inspirational leadership of staff? Work-based learners have the opportunity to develop communication skills within their studies to address these moments – look at the inclusion of key terms such as 'sustained, shared thinking' and the way it has become embedded in early years documentation and hopefully practice.

Action research developed through the work of, among others, Kurt Lewin in the 1940s, who researched what happened when people became involved in the decision-making processes within their work situations. Many researchers, especially within education, developed his ideas and organized their work into a cyclical process: observe, reflect, act, evaluate, and modify (McNiff and Whitehead 2006: 9).

A practitioner may, for example, *observe* a small group of children showing an interest in each other's hair. On *reflection*, links could be made with the living projects of Reggio Emilia and the potential for a holistic, child-initiated approach to learning and development. *Action* could involve entering a discussion with the children about hair and developing together activities such as finding different types of hair, hair care, creating a role play area such as a hair salon indoors and outdoors, and reading and writing activities. Always be open to the unexpected and include it! *Evaluation* can link with government legislation, such as identifying the cross-curricular areas of learning covered within the Early Years Foundation Stage (DCSF 2007) as well as demonstration of 'sustained shared thinking' in relation to quality practice. *Modify* will address how this learning experience may be adapted or developed for future practice. Data can be collected throughout the process by such methods as video recording, photography, observation, and samples of children's work. Evidence is then selected from the collected data to demonstrate the learning that has occurred in relation to the chosen question for all participants, including oneself.

Within an action-research cycle it is important to identify the baseline of what 'is' and plan from evidence readily available arising from observations, current records, evaluations of activities or meetings. Obviously the issue of confidentiality is key from the start and may influence the choice of material available for evidence. Even when using pseudonyms/codes for different people and places involved, there remains the ethical importance of seeing all as active participants in the research.

Ethical statements, which allow for transparency, need to be completed at the start (see Appendix 3). If photos or video material are likely to be used, then state this within the ethical statement. State also how/if this material will be disposed of/archived at the end of the research. Check with the workplace policies and qualification awarding body, as often no faces should be shown. This is frustrating for students who want to demonstrate emotional responses, but acknowledgement of the rights of the individual is essential. Alison Clark (2004), through use of the mosaic approach, found ways for the voices of children to be heard while acknowledging their rights, leaving plenty of scope for development.

A key concern about the use of qualitative research, as opposed to quantitative research, has been the validity of the knowledge gained, when inevitably it involves subjective activity and decision making. 'I' as practitioner will influence the whole process. Triangulation is a way of strengthening validity through collecting different types of data that can be used as evidence – observations by different people, photographs, children's work, interviews – which can enable the researcher to compare and combine findings from different sources (Roberts-Holmes 2005: 40). To move beyond, while still acknowledging, the 'I', choose one or two 'critical friends'. These are individuals who may have some knowledge of what you are trying to do (peers, colleagues, parents) and will be prepared actively to listen to and critically question you throughout the period of research. This adds another 'third party' or more to the research process, providing additional perspectives and enriching the findings (McNiff and Whitehead 2006: 85).

When the foundations are laid, as above, it is also worth considering the skills of the researcher and those around when choosing what evidence to collect. Different types of evidence require different skills, all of which can be learnt, but restraints on time may determine how much new ground can be covered within each piece of research. Over a two- to three-year study period, there will be time to build these up within different assignments.

Consider Table 7.1 when identifying the skills against the type of evidence.

Table 7.1 Identifying skills against the type of evidence

Type of evidence	Skills I need	Reasons for choice
Records of planning, monitoring, and assessment	• Ability to record using sheets that acknowledge the Early Years Foundation Stage (DCSF 2007) • Familiarity with different types of assessment – formative and summative. • Confidence to ask for consent of participants – relative to age – and access to plans	• Provision of baseline • Evidence of use of the planning cycle • Learning and development links to government guidelines • Evidence of personalized learning
Observations of implementation of activity	• Willingness to observe and listen with total concentration – 'drown in observation', 'total immersion' • Ability to keep an open mind • Collaboration with team members who may submit observed evidence • Competence with different ways of recording observations – event sampling, naturalistic • Ability to select from above data to provide the best/most valid evidence to address the research topic • Ability to include enough children to allow for sickness, reluctance to be involved • Time management skills – to observe, write up, reflect and evaluate	• Evidence of what did happen • Can take into account the unexpected • Provides information for future planning • Provides information for assessment • Direct way to learn about child development • Can provide 'triangulation' by using different types of observation alongside other methods, helping to validate data

Type of evidence	Skills I need	Reasons for choice
Observations of 'free-flow' play	• Choose the form of observation with care and justify the reason for your choice – 'look, listen, note', naturalistic/ descriptive, mapping • Ability to move with the children • Flexible timing to stay with the process • Skills to write 'verbatim' recording all that is said, including sounds for babies	• Evidence of what did happen • Can take into account the unexpected • Provides information for future planning • Provides information for assessment • Direct way to learn about child development and individual interests
Observation of meetings with: • Parents • Staff • Other professionals	• To be seen as trustworthy • Keen listening skills • Capable of recording verbatim • Confidence to ask afterwards if unsure of meanings • Willingness to learn from others and record other viewpoints to bring about potential change	• Evidence of skills required for parent partnership and multi-agency/multi-disciplinary working • Inclusion of other 'voices'/ideas which add to discovery within research process triangulation, adding to validity of research
Interviews with: • Child/children • Parents • Staff • Other professionals	• Knowledge of the rights of the child and adult and recognition of application of this knowledge, including safeguarding guidelines • Ability to acquire informed consent and set boundaries for confidentiality • To create relevant, concise, open-ended questions specific to the topic and age appropriate • Warm, inviting approach • Time management skills that value the age/ability of the interviewee	• Direct verbal responses • Access to specific information/knowledge • Different viewpoints/ ideas can be heard • Triangulation, adding to validity of research.

Type of evidence	Skills I need	Reasons for choice
	• Active listening skills • Ability to read body language • Empathy • Possible translation	
• Photographs • Video recordings	• Use of digital camera(s) • Printing/scanning • Obtaining consent of participants • Selection of a 'photographer', including children • Ability to work with the 'photographer' • Deciding on the level of 'freedom' for the photographer • Recognition of effect of use of the 'tool' on the outcome/validity of the research	• 'Real-world' evidence • Recognition of 'active participation' by others within research, leading to increased sense of ownership by the wider community • 'Open dialogue'
Collections of children's work	• Skills to obtain consent from participants • Photocopying/scanning • Safe-keeping/confidentiality • Acknowledgement of how any why the selection of work took place in direct relation to the research topic • Recognition of ethical response to 'rewards' for children's work and their implication, e.g. impact on child of recognition of inclusion in research or of any gifts offered	• Clear visual data • Autonomy/originality • Material for analysis

Types of observations

It is always important to remember the impact of the observer(s) on the outcome of what is being observed. A conscious decision should be made as to whether the observer(s) will be taking a direct part (participant observer) or will stand back and watch from a distance (non-participant observer). Even with the latter, children and adults are likely to be aware of the concentration of someone else on what they are doing, so note this when writing up the research.

Choices can be made from the following:

- naturalistic, descriptive;
- look, listen, note – valuing everyday recording of individual achievement to add to a child's profile of learning and development;
- event sampling;
- running record – identifying the specific behaviour related to the research;
- tally counting;
- observation schedules – provide a structure of specific questions to answer that maintain the focus on a child or group of children (Lancaster and Broadbent, in Roberts-Holmes 2003: 98);
- the Tavistock Method adapted for use in early years settings (Elfer 2005: 120) and shared within a supportive group, possibly other early years practitioners.

The subjective element of qualitative research is inevitable and needs to be acknowledged. Work-based practitioner learners who have been introduced to the Tavistock Method have appreciated being able to immerse themselves for 10–20 minutes in watching a young child without writing. They aim to tap into the emotions within the experience as well as the observational details. After this time they write freely about all they remember in the order things occurred. The written observation is shared and discussed with colleagues or the supervisor, acknowledging different outlooks on the events. The practitioner continues to observe and record, returning to the group with updates for discussion. As Elfer (2005: 120) states: 'At the heart of this method of observation lies the fact that we are able not only to *see* and *hear* the reactions and responses of another person but also have the capacity to have feelings evoked in us by another person'.

This tends to ring true for education and childcare practitioners. Think of the emotions evoked in seeing a baby smile for the first time or the teardrops starting to role down young children's faces when they realize their parent has left. This method has primarily been introduced with under-threes, but with the potential development of early years 'learning communities' there may be more scope for use by early years practitioners throughout the Early Years Foundation Stage.

Each individual piece of research will have to meet deadlines. Students who devise a research planner/timeline at the start will be able to plan how they will collect their evidence in relation to other key work-based and personal events (see sample below). This will impact on the final choice of evidence. As some practitioners have to turn round assignments requiring practitioner research within four weeks, the timeline has been created with this in mind but can be extended. A crucial factor is remembering that the collection of evidence provides information for the reflection, analysis, and evaluation of evidence. Leaving time to write up and sift through the evidence to select the key issues relating to the research question is crucial. Working backwards from the deadline, allowing this time, may seem illogical but is essential. Individuals discover their own 'routines' for completing practitioner research. A more detailed planner will say specifically when each item is to be carried out, plus as Cottrell (2003: 83) suggests, allot how long each will take, then record how long it actually took. This provides a monitoring record for personal development, identifying progression during a period of study as research skills develop.

Research planner/timeline

Planning – Week 1

1. **Establish the research question.** Highlight keywords in the research question/assignment and check your understanding with others so that you are clear about what will be required. Write reflective journal/log.
2. **Identify specific knowledge and resources** from previous studies relating to this topic. Start to create your *bibliography* as you begin background reading. Look for references in these familiar texts to follow up and extend your reading. Combine with any carefully selected current lecture/workshop materials and internet searches on keywords and relevant theories.
3. **Choose research methods** that you are comfortable with, using available sources to provide the best evidence for your topic within the time scale. Your selection may be influenced by your background reading, drawing on the work of other work-based learners/ researchers.
4. **Create a list of active participants** – adults and children. State how (written/verbal) and when you will inform them about the

research, gaining evidence of their willingness to be involved – ethical statement (see sample). You may choose to involve a 'critical friend' to discuss the process with and to offer different perspectives.

5. **Identify other resources required, creating materials as needed** – such as equipment, planning sheets, observation records, interview questions. Include agreed dates and times for implementation.

Implementation – Week 2/3

6. **Gain informed consent from active participants** – collect and retain evidence.
7. **Carry out the planned action at the agreed times** – complete observations of the 'action' plus records of interviews or meetings.

Reflect and Evaluate – Week 3/4

8. **Reflect on collected evidence** – reflect as you write up observations, display collected work, photos/videos, transcribe interviews/meetings. Maintain reflective journal entries. Look for links with knowledge and theories from background reading
9. **Critically analyse the evidence** in relation to the relevant theories, government documentation, and international perspectives. Type as you go.
10. **Evaluate the research process** – identify the learning, strengths, and areas for development, including the next steps arising from the research.

Writing up – Week 4

11. **Organize the content.** Select the key evidence, reflections, and critical analytical thoughts. Group the information so that it presents the strongest evidence for your research question. Use *appendices* to display relevant summaries of data.
12. **Write up.** Create an initial draft with a clear *introduction* and *conclusion*. Check whether an *abstract* – brief summary of the research and findings placed at the beginning – is required. Read through, thinking about ways to improve. Check all specific criteria are met. Write up *references/bibliography*. Complete the final copy. Proof-read. Hand in, with all required formal paperwork, to meet deadline.

How will I judge if I am successful?

The strength of practitioner research is that the process is regarded as worthwhile if the procedures mentioned above are adhered to. The *reliability* of the evidence and presentation need to be demonstrated by transparency. Never assume the reader knows what may appear to you to be basic; instead aim to include details within plans, written observations and records, and ethical statements. Make sure you can justify why you have chosen the methodology you have – the type of observation, the choice of participants and activity. The *validity* of your research can be demonstrated through using a variety of evidence, showing triangulation.

Allowing time for honest reflection, critical thinking, and evaluation will lead to evidence of learning in the written research that will be grounded in relevant theory and effective early years practice. Success may be demonstrated by the obvious constructive learning and development that has occurred for participants – adults (including self) and children – and the potential for others to learn from the experience to improve practice.

However, within work-based learning, the practitioner research process may identify concerns that are not always considered 'successful'. This will then depend on the reflective practice, critical thinking, compelling evidence, and evaluation to identify areas for potential change. Planning for improvements can then lead to 'success', with the practitioner researcher being an *agent for change*. It might be that success is seen more through sound documentation of each individual research experience adding to the pool of evidence of early years practice.

Key areas for the future

Compared with health and social care, early childhood education and care is a relatively new area for study. David *et al.* (2005: 52) identified particular areas in relation to 'Birth to Three Matters' that require research:

- toddlers in early childhood care and education settings;
- the impact of practitioner training on the experiences of children and parents;
- links between early years care and education provision and parental employment, especially from the child's point of view.

According to the British Educational Research Association Early Years Special Interest Group, other gaps include:

- young children's learning in the arts, humanities, physical education

or spiritual and moral education in early childhood education and care settings;
• outcomes for children of different types of staff training.

Seminar groups allow for students to share the process of their research. There might also be opportunities for sharing the results of the varied projects that are being carried out, linking practitioners with common interests. These interests often spark commitment for further research within Masters programmes and beyond. There remains the potential for learning communities to become established through early years professional networks, possibly including work-based learners on other programmes. The way research has influenced national practice has become clear, so the doorway is open as the required skills develop. This form of individual and group learning should then continue to drive quality provision for learning, development, and welfare in the early years as adults and children enjoy and achieve together.

References

Clark, A. (2004) The mosaic approach and research with young children, in V. Lewis, M. Kellett, C. Robinson, S. Fraser and S. Ding (eds) *The Reality of Research with Children and Young People*. London: Sage Publications in association with Open University Press.

Cottrell, S. (2003) *The Study Skills Handbook* (2nd edn). Basingstoke: Palgrave Macmillan.

David, T., Goouch, K. and Powell, S. (2005) Research matters, in L. Abbott and A. Langston (eds) *Birth to Three Matters: Supporting the Framework of Effective Practice*. Maidenhead: Open University Press.

Department for Children, Schools and Families (2007) *Early Years Foundation Stage*. London: DCSF.

Elfer, P. (2005) Observation matters, in L. Abbott and A. Langston (eds) *Birth to Three Matters: Supporting the Framework of Effective Practice*. Maidenhead: Open University Press.

Haywood Metz, M. and Page, R.N. (2002) The uses of practitioner research and status issues in educational research: reply to Gary Anderson, *Educational Researcher*, 31(7): 26–7.

McNiff, J. and Whitehead, J. (2006) *All You Need to Know about Action Research*. London: Sage Publications.

Roberts-Holmes, G. (2005) *Doing your Early Years Research Project: A Step-by-step Guide*. London: Paul Chapman Publishing.

Robson, C. (1993) *Real World Research: A Resource for Social Scientists and Practitioner-researchers*. Oxford: Blackwell.

PART 3
IMPACT

8 My learning journey: practitioners' perspectives

We don't receive wisdom; we must discover it for ourselves after a journey that no one can take for us or spare us.

Marcel Proust (1871–1922)

For many early years practitioners, setting out on a learning journey, often after a long break from studying, can seem like climbing a mountain in trainers! It is my experience after working with mature students on a variety of early years courses that they are the most dedicated and hard-working professionals. Like any practitioner, the outcomes of working alongside avid learners can be extremely rewarding. The role of a university lecturer/facilitator is to provide opportunities within a learning community for practitioners to reach beyond competence and proficiency and to strive to achieve excellence in practice. This is a lifelong journey and can present many choices, but once the decision to learn more has been made there is little doubt that it can be life changing. The benefits of learning alongside others can be supportive, challenging, and thought-provoking. Other benefits include:

- peer support;
- developing life-long friendships;
- fostering a love of learning;
- engendering a spirit of 'togetherness';
- creating a professional network;
- sharing of expertise.

This final chapter pulls together the strands that work-based learners experience emotionally, academically, personally, and professionally. Many have gone on to become mentors for others following in their footsteps. Early years practitioners can extend and build on their expertise, exchange their views, and share good practice if well supported. Universities, colleges, practitioners, and all partners have a responsibility towards enabling and recognizing hard-won achievements. When reading through the learning journeys below, it is clear that the journey for some has just begun. There is a realization that they can be independent learners and researchers. That they can take responsibility for taking their own expertise further and begin to influence and be part of a wider learning research community. Many have spoken about how they are able to challenge and question many issues and concerns put before them in a non-confrontational way. They are able to articulate their concerns or views about critical issues that arise. Most of all they talk about how they are able to access and collect compelling evidence gained from consistent and informed good practice. This in turn has given them the confidence to evaluate their careers and apply for posts they had in the past dismissed. Some have gone on to further their qualifications and at last acknowledged their increased academic, personal, and professional abilities.

The following stories will hopefully inspire those reading them to feel supported and that there is someone out there who has also struggled with their insecurities of working and doing academic study. The stories demonstrate that it does take perseverance, organization, and self-confidence but that the learning journey is worthwhile.

Dolly Walker – my learning journey

When I enrolled on the foundation degree course I had mixed emotions. I was excited because I was facing a new challenge but I was also worried about studying again. The self-doubts about finding the time to do the course and actually being able to work to a high enough standard were constantly on my mind. However, with a full bursary to pay my fees and the chance to develop myself further, it was an opportunity too good to miss.

Going to college each week was not a chore, I enjoyed the lectures, group discussions, and exercises. Assignment writing was always difficult to fit in, but it had to be done, so I managed it. On our 'hand-in' days we would go around the class to see who had stayed up the latest to complete their assignment. I think four o'clock in the morning was the latest ever! The camaraderie we had was fantastic and I was lucky enough to have several friends who supported me and gave advice when I had 'writer's block' at assignment time. Although I was a reflective practitioner who modelled good practice, when I started the course I learnt so much during this time that everyone in my setting (children, staff, and parents) all benefited from it.

After my foundation degree I chose to undertake a BA (Hons) degree in early years education and childcare. Again, I was worried about the standard of writing I would have to achieve and I didn't know if I could face another year of study. I'm so glad that I did stay on, as the year actually went by quickly and was again beneficial to my practice and myself. This final year of study made me much more of an independent learner and I think that will stay with me forever. I went to the Barbican for my graduation day and it was one of the best days of my life.

During my studies, we obviously talked about new developments within the early year's field so early years professional status was a familiar subject. When Kingston ran the pilot programme for early years professional status, I had no hesitation in enrolling. I firmly believed that this was the status to which practitioners in early years should aspire. Also, after three years of study there would be no better time to do it. While there were written tasks to complete and assessment days, they were all achievable, as I was writing and talking about my own working practice and experiences. I found that the early years professional status programme enabled me to prove and demonstrate my knowledge and understanding of early years at the highest level.

A few months after I achieved early years professional status, I saw a job advertised within my local authority for a workforce development officer. I applied for the post and was appointed. I have absolutely no doubt that the training I had undertaken played a major part in my success. I believe passionately in raising the qualification levels of practitioners, as in time this will help raise the profile and status of early years workers. They have been overlooked for too long and now is the time for that to change. The hard work and responsibilities that are taken on daily by early years workers are finally being recognized by the government, and practitioners now have a clear career path to follow if they wish. In my new post I hope I will be able to advise and support many practitioners who would like to further their career or study to improve their practice.

On a personal level, I know the training I have completed has made me more confident with all aspects of my life. I have also had great personal as well as professional satisfaction when completing each of my study programmes.

Jacky Brewer – my learning journey

I am a natural nurturer. As a child I always protected anything living, from cranefly to children. My upbringing in a rural community helped me to develop a deep respect for life. I didn't have a choice about going into further education, as my mother strongly believed it was wasted on girls. As soon as I celebrated my sixteenth birthday, I was expected to contribute to the household budget. I knew I was capable of more; I can vaguely remember teachers fighting my cause to stay on at school, but I eventually left without qualifications.

The first position I found was as a live-in assistant matron in a boys' boarding school. The boys started at five or six years of age and many of their parents were overseas. Many times during my stay the teaching staff would tell me the boys were calmer since I had started to look after them. If only they knew, I was as homesick as they were. During the 1970s, the numbers of boarders dropped and the school started to receive day children, so after a year I had to leave.

The manager of a local swimming pool knew me and offered me a position as a lifeguard. I worked for the local authority for nearly twenty years in various roles. During the early 1980s, I became a member of the management team of a leisure centre in a deprived area. My role involved dealing with members of the public, running children's courses and staff teams of up to thirty people. As the only female member of the leisure management team, I was deemed qualified to start a crèche for children of parents using the leisure facilities. These were in the pre-legislation days, so I had to use my life experience to guide me. On reflection, I didn't do too badly. I employed parents of children I had worked with in the centre so knew their history and I had very fixed ideas about safety and hygiene. I also wanted to do something about the children wandering around the local housing estate. During one particularly harsh winter, I set up a Saturday club that then developed into a holiday club using the leisure centre facilities. I received great resistance from the rest of the management team; it meant more work for them. If a child told me he could not pay, I would check his pockets and it became known that children living in a particular area would receive a swim, a team game, a hot drink, and a doughnut for as little as one penny. Both clubs grew in popularity until the local authority recognized it as a profit centre and took control. The locality of this leisure centre became one of the first areas recognized to be in need of a children's centre.

When I became pregnant nobody knew what to do with me [in the workplace]. It was around this time that committees were formed to develop British Safety Standards for children, so I was given 'free rein' to attend meetings and join committees that supported this legislation. We discussed anything and everything regarding safety around children, from car seatbelts and toys to adult/child ratios. It was during this time that I knew I would work in childcare.

After having my second child, I avidly read childcare books. I worked part-time within the leisure industry and my husband shared the childcare. I used this time to access the diploma of pre-school practice.

Once my children started school, I worked in a pre-school attached to a maintained primary school, then eventually went to work for a preparatory school, where I worked in the nursery, kindergarten, and reception. This school had a very strong ethos that ensured the staff made learning fun. In my view, the motto 'Happy Children Learn' was quite perceptive. The new reception teacher inspired me with her methods of teaching. Class worksheets came last; if all else was in place, then they were used as an extension activity. After a few years the school closed and merged with another preparatory school. This was a very unhappy place; the staff were inadequately trained and led by the governors, parents, and other staff who expected children to access a curriculum, which, in my view, was inappropriate.

I left and took the post of supervisor of a committee-managed pre-school within a shared setting. What an eye-opener! With the Ten Year Strategy in its infancy and only a childcare magazine to inform me of its expectations, it was with great relief I learnt of the early years foundation degree. My participation was made possible by the package of funding provided by the local authority Early Years Development and Childcare Partnership Department and Kingston University. It was a life-changing opportunity for me.

By the second year of the early years foundation degree, I felt I had outgrown my setting. As a committee-managed pre-school in a close-knit rural community, I felt frustrated at the lack of understanding or commitment from the members. I experienced great resistance at every turn, so before I left I put a recommendation to the committee that they should explore the possibility of integrating the setting with the local mainstream school and a practitioner accessing her first year of the early years foundation degree.

During my three years of study at Kingston University, I developed in-depth knowledge and understanding of the early years and specialized in the subject of transition and outdoor learning. As a student, I contributed in a small way to the Early Years Foundation Stage and worked at improving parental and community involvement at settings where I practised. Both parents and community are important in the delivery of the 'Every Child Matters' legislation.

I have journeyed full circle and currently teach a reception class that shares the early years unit. My teaching style has changed radically since that first reception class in the early 1990s. My practice during the academic year 2006–7 saw the whole curriculum for reception as 'play based'. I recently celebrated success following the considerable efforts I and my colleague put into my current setting by being recognized by OfSTED as an 'outstanding' setting during October 2006.

Without my life skills and professional development gained, the lectures and short courses I have attended and the knowledge I have gained from the children I work with, this achievement would not have been possible.

A tutor recently inspired me to look at my everyday practice and introduce value-added activities to our daily routine. Following this a childcare magazine now wants me to write an article on our good practice in mathematics.

I am once again in a community that echoes my childhood and feel that with the importance of outdoor learning I am able to make a significant impact on the lives of the children and families that use this setting. In my current setting, I have recognized that there is a community that we do not do enough to support, so I am accessing an MA to further enhance my knowledge and understanding of the ethnicity of the community this setting supports.

Have I reached the end of my learning journey? I feel as if I have only just started. I have mentored six practitioners who are accessing a range of qualifications from NVQ3 to BA (Hons), which in turn supports their settings. Once I am through my early years professional status I will be in a position to mentor the next wave through. Where do I go from here? I feel drawn to teach adults, to inspire them to develop their knowledge and understanding in a subject that is unfolding at this time. I want to motivate and inspire as I have been by several of the teachers, tutors and lecturers I have had the privilege to learn from over the years.

I feel frustrated that I started down the higher education journey well into my forties. I deal with it by thinking about the following analogy. I am the tip of a pyramid. I have mentored six practitioners. I hope that, through example, these six will see the benefits of mentoring others themselves, and at each stage, with shared knowledge and practice, they should by evolution reach higher standards than I have. Once I started thinking about the concept of this for just one mentor, the possibilities of what will be achieved have become awesome!

Zoë Hale – a talk at the Children's Workforce Development Council celebration evening

My name is Zoë Hale, I am the early support coordinator for the London Borough of Walthamstow. I am also happy to say I have gained early years professional status.

My learning journey

I have always worked within the early years going back twenty-two years. The positions I have held include being a nursery nurse, nanny, as well as a children's club representative living in Spain for two years. What fun!

After becoming a mother (I have two daughters aged seventeen and fourteen), I became involved in my local pre-school. This is where I found my passion for working with children with disabilities and special educational needs.

From pre-school I moved into school, working as a nursery officer/special needs assistant. This is where my journey back into education began. I completed a year-long course, gaining a Level 3 NCFE national award for special needs assistants. During my time in school, my manager and head teacher informed me of the opportunity to gain a foundation degree through Kingston University. Though I thought there was no way I was degree material! As the course was to be delivered locally, I guessed there was no harm in applying. My theory being if I got through the interview, I would give it a go.

Luckily I got in! As the degree was work based it fitted in perfectly with my busy life. My time management is much improved as a result! During my first year on the course, I decided to stick with my passion for special educational needs, and made the difficult decision to leave the mainstream school I had spent nine happy years in and apply for a post as a portage worker. This decision made some of my assignments problematic, but my tutors were very supportive and guided me through.

I continued in this role for the duration of my degree. After completing the foundation degree, I went on to complete the progression year to gain a BA (Hons) degree in early years education and childcare, in which I got a first-class honours degree! I was also overwhelmed to receive the Lillian De Lissa award for outstanding practice.

During the final stages of my degree, the Kingston tutors informed us of this long-waited-for status. At this time, my peers and I named ourselves the 'pilot princesses', as the foundation degree, the progression routes BA, and now the early years professional status route were all pilot pathways. I must admit after three years of hard slog, I was not too keen!

After lots of support and guidance from Kingston, I started on the validation route. The process was fairly painless, I even enjoyed the group exercises and staff interview at the gateway review!

Where do I start? Well I would not be here today if I had not gone through the whole process of the foundation degree, honours degree, and now early years professional status. I would never have had the confidence to do this previously. My role as early support coordinator is a management position, so the journey I have been through has given me the skills and knowledge needed to roll out early support across the borough. I liaise with early years settings and children's centres as well as professionals from all agencies across the borough, so having my background and now the early years professional status gives me the ability to undertake my role with confidence. I also deliver training to early years practitioners across all agencies.

During the journey I have made friends and contacts that have been so valuable in my role as we have been able to link up and work together. We are working closely with Waltham Forest's quality and training advisor to promote early years professional status, including open days and seminars across the borough. We also have a mini-forum (just the four of us at the moment, but hopefully that will grow), which enables us to support each other in practice.

That just leaves me to say 'thank you' for inviting me here tonight, and I would like you to remember that not only does every child matter, every early years professional does too!

Conclusion

I hope these learning journeys inspire those of you who are thinking that you would like to develop personally and professionally. Each of the above journeys demonstrates that roles and responsibilities are developing and being created in response to the changing face of the children's workforce. You will be the agents of change and for change.

Appendices

Appendix 1: definitions of those involved with integrated services

Care trusts within the UK National Health Service (NHS) are organizations that work in both health and social care. They carry out a range of services, including social care, mental health services, and primary care services. Care trusts are set up when the NHS and local authorities agree to work closely together, usually where it is felt that a closer relationship between health and social care is needed or would benefit local care services.

Child protection officer – an individual responsible for coordinating policy and action on safeguarding children.

Children's Workforce Development Council (CWDC) – the CWDC exists to improve the lives of children, young people, their families, and carers by ensuring that all people working with them have the best possible training, qualifications, support, and advice. It also helps children's and young people's organizations and services to work together better so that the child is at the centre of all services.

Clinical psychologist – someone who works in the areas of personality assessment and prevention and treatment of emotional and mental disorders. Clinical psychologists usually work with individuals, groups or families who have personal, social, emotional or behavioural problems.

Department for Children, Schools, and Families (DCFS) – leads work across government to ensure that all children and young people:

- remain healthy and safe;
- secure an excellent education and the highest possible standards of achievement;
- enjoy their childhood;
- make a positive contribution to society and the economy; and
- have lives full of opportunity, free from the effects of poverty.

Department of Health – a department of the British Government. It is led by the Secretary of State for Health with two junior Ministers of State. It is responsible for healthcare policies and providing basic healthcare services.

Educational psychologist – a person, usually employed by the local authority, whose training and experience focus on using psychological theory to assess children with learning difficulties, then advise on their development and educational progress.

Family support worker – a family support worker assists families who are experiencing problems, visiting them regularly to offer practical help and emotional support. The aim is to allow children to remain with their families rather than being taken into care.

Foster carer – a key person responsible for substitute care, usually in a home licensed by a public agency, for children whose welfare requires removal from their homes.

Heath visitor – a health visitor is a registered nurse who has undertaken further training to provide health education and preventative care for children under five years. Some may also specialize in school health and preventative care of the elderly.

Local authorities are administrative units of local government with a responsibility to fulfil statutory requirements.

Occupational therapist – a health professional trained to help people who are ill or disabled to learn to manage their daily activities. A therapist who specializes in child development will evaluate a child's skills, especially in the areas of fine motor and eye–hand coordination, and general development. The occupational therapist can assist the child in daily living skills and is mainly concerned with hand strength and use of the arms and hands.

Physiotherapist – a physiotherapist is a healthcare professional who assesses physical function and helps to restore and maintain as normal a function as possible. Physiotherapists can treat physical disorders through manipulation, mobilization techniques, and by prescribing strengthening exercises and advice where appropriate.

Portage worker – someone who works with the learning disabilities service, and has particular expertise in working with parents of pre-school children, helping them with developmental difficulties using a home teaching method.

Primary care trust – many NHS services in the UK are provided by NHS trusts. There are two major types of trusts: primary care trusts and hospital trusts.

Social worker – a professional trained to talk with people and their families about emotional or physical needs, and to find them support services. They monitor and assist the social, emotional, and psychological growth and development of a child and his or her family.

Speech and language therapist – an individual who works with children who have problems with speech development to help them overcome their communication difficulties. They also can assess and manage difficulties with eating and swallowing. The speech and language therapist also deals with communication difficulties.

SureStart is a cross-government programme of support for children under four and their families living in deprived areas. It aims to ensure that all children are ready to learn when they arrive at school. Funding is focused on improving opportunities and facilities available to this group.

Training and Development Agency (TDA) – this agency works with schools to develop the workforce and to ensure that schools can recruit good-quality, well-trained people. It supports schools to provide extended services for parents, children, and young people.

Appendix 2

	Knowledge and understanding *Candidates for Early Years Professional Status (EYPS) must demonstrate through their practice that a secure knowledge and understanding of the following underpins their own practice and informs their leadership of others.*
1	The principles and content of the Early Years Foundation Stage and how to put them into practice.
S2	The individual and diverse ways in which children develop and learn from birth to the end of the Foundation Stage and thereafter.
S3	How children's well-being, development, learning, and behaviour can be affected by a range of influences and transitions from inside and outside the setting.
S4	The main provisions of the national and local statutory and non-statutory frameworks within which children's services work and their implications for early years settings.
S5	The current legal requirements, national policies, and guidance on health and safety, safeguarding and promoting the well being of children, and their implications for early years settings.
S6	The contribution that other professionals within the setting and beyond can make to children's physical and emotional well-being, development, and learning.

	Effective practice *Candidates for EYPS must demonstrate through their practice that they meet all the following standards and that they can lead and support others to:*
S7	Have high expectations of all children and commitment to ensuring that they can achieve their full potential.
S8	Establish and sustain a safe, welcoming, purposeful, stimulating, and encouraging environment where children feel confident and secure and are able to develop and learn.
S9	Provide balanced and flexible daily and weekly routines that meet children's needs and enable them to develop and learn.
S10	Use close, informed observation and other strategies to monitor children's activity, development, and progress systematically and carefully, and use this information to inform, plan, and improve practice and provision.
S11	Plan and provide safe and appropriate child-led and adult-initiated experiences, activities, and play opportunities in indoor and outdoor and in out-of-setting contexts, which enable children to develop and learn.

S12	Select, prepare, and use a range of resources suitable for children's ages, interests, and abilities, taking account of diversity and promoting equality and inclusion.
S13	Make effective personalized provision for the children they work with.
S14	Respond appropriately to children, informed by how children develop and learn and a clear understanding of possible next steps in their development and learning.
S15	Support the development of children's language and communication skills.
S16	Engage in sustained shared thinking with children.
S17	Promote positive behaviour, self-control, and independence through using effective behaviour management strategies and developing children's social, emotional, and behavioural skills.
S18	Promote children's rights, equality, inclusion, and anti-discriminatory practice in all aspects of their practice.
S19	Establish a safe environment and employ practices that promote children's health, safety and physical, mental, and emotional well-being.
S20	Recognize when children are in danger or at risk of harm and know how to act to protect them.
S21	Assess, record, and report on progress in children's development and learning and use this as a basis for differentiating provision.
S22	Give constructive and sensitive feedback to help children understand what they have achieved and think about what they need to do next and, when appropriate, encourage children to think about, evaluate, and improve on their own performance.
S23	Identify and support children whose progress, development or well-being is affected by changes or difficulties in their personal circumstances and know when to refer them to colleagues for specialist support.
S24	Be accountable for the delivery of high-quality provision.

Relationships with children

Candidates for EYPS must demonstrate through their practice that they meet all the following standards and that they can lead and support others to:

S25	Establish fair, respectful, trusting, supportive, and constructive relationships with children.
S26	Communicate sensitively and effectively with children from birth to the end of the Foundation Stage.
S27	Listen to children, pay attention to what they say, and value and respect their views.
S28	Demonstrate the positive values, attitudes, and behaviour they expect from children.

Communicating and working in partnership with families and carers

Candidates for EYPS must demonstrate through their practice that they meet all the following standards and that they can lead and support others to:

S29	Recognize and respect the influential and enduring contribution that families and parents/carers can make to children's development, well-being, and learning.
S30	Establish fair, respectful, trusting, and constructive relationships with families and parents/carers, and communicate sensitively and effectively with them.
S31	Work in partnership with families and parents/carers, at home and in the setting, to nurture children, to help them develop, and to improve outcomes for them.
S32	Provide formal and informal opportunities through which information about children's well-being, development, and learning can be shared between the setting and families and parents/carers.

Teamwork and collaboration

Candidates for EYPS must demonstrate that they:

S33	Establish and sustain a culture of collaborative and cooperative working between colleagues.
S34	Ensure that colleagues working with them understand their role and are involved appropriately in helping children to meet planned objectives.
S35	Influence and shape the policies and practices of the setting and share in collective responsibility for their implementation.
S36	Contribute to the work of a multi-professional team and, where appropriate, coordinate and implement agreed programmes and interventions on a day-to-day basis.

Professional development	
Candidates for EYPS must demonstrate through their practice that they meet all the following standards and that they can lead and support others to:	
S37	Develop and use skills in literacy, numeracy, and information and communication technology to support their work with children and wider professional activities.
S38	Reflect on and evaluate the impact of practice, modifying approaches where necessary, and take responsibility for identifying and meeting their professional development needs.
S39	Take a creative and constructively critical approach towards innovation, and adapt practice if benefits and improvements are identified.

Source: Children's Workforce and Development Council (2006) CWDC Handbook. London: CWDC.

Appendix 3

Title of Course ....

Ethical Statement

I am undertaking a .... course at .... that involves the study of children operating at, or within, the 0–5 year old age range. I will be studying a wide range of topics around early years practice and conducting small-scale research projects concerned with **enhancing my own professional practice.**

I would be grateful if you would allow me to include my observations and assessments of your child in my work, and could confirm this by signing the slip below. The following statements provide professional and ethical guidelines for my work.

- The findings will be incorporated into my assignments, which will form part of my degree portfolio. Once the study has been assessed, a copy of my work will be kept for reference purposes only.
- The school's and participants' anonymity will be safeguarded. For the purposes of my studies, pseudonyms will be used throughout.
- All transcripts of conversations will be signed by the participants to indicate their approval of the transcripts' use and to confirm that they are a true record of the conversation.
- Any records, questionnaires, and other evidence will be kept in a secure environment and will not be made available to other persons apart from staff connected with the course.
- The head teacher/manager has given permission for me to follow this course, and is aware that I will be using data collected from children in my care.
- I am being supported by tutors and a mentor throughout the duration of the course and they will guide me in the appropriate collection and use of my findings.
- After the final assessment of my course, the archived material will be destroyed.

....

(Student: Please tear off this slip after the parent/carer has signed and dated it and keep it in a safe place)

I give permission for data relevant to my son/daughter to be used for the purposes of your studies. I may withdraw my permission at any time.

Child's Name: _____

Signed Parent/Carer: _____ Date:

Student's Name: _____ Date:

Manager's/Head teacher's name: _____ Date:

Index

Locators shown in *italics* refer to tables, boxes, diagrams and student activities.

Abbott, L., 72
action research, 111–12
Adonis, A., 94
agencies, multiple
  characteristics and impact of collaboration patterns and trends, 35–7
  exercise involving responses of, 85–90
  exercise on use of concern-issue-conflict involving, 84–5
  need and importance, 82–4
  see also partnerships, multiple agency
Ainsworth, M., 58–9
Airey, S., 100
All Our Futures (1999), 71
Athey, C., 55
attitudes, child learning
  salience in early years environments, 99–103, *101*
auditory learners, 51
autonomy
  salience in relation to children and learning environments, 66–8

Bandura, A., 58–9
beliefs, early-year practitioner
  salience in relation to early years and learning environments, 62–6, *62, 63, 64, 65, 66*
BERA (British Education Research Association), 67, 71, 119–20
Bettelheim, B., 21–2
bibliographies
  characteristics and writing of, 48–50, *49–50*
  see also references and referencing
Birth to Three Matters: Change for Children (2003), 34–5
Bousted, M., 6
Bowers, S., 15

Bowlby, J., 58–9
Brewer, J. (case study)
  experiences as early years learning student, 125–8
British Education Research Association (BERA), 67, 71, 119–20
Bruce, T., 57–8
Bruner, J, 29–30, 57–8

CAF (Common Assessment Framework), 81–2
Call, J., 63
Campbell, J., 19
Canella, G., 18
Carpenter, M., 63
Carr, M., 69, 102
case studies
  early years student practitioner-learner experiences, 124–30
CEHR (Commission for Equality and Human Rights), 71–2
Childcare Act (2006), 79, 80–81, 85
children
  importance of autonomy and respect for, 66–8
  see also cultures, child
Children's Plan (2007) 15
Children's Workforce Development Council (CWDC), 15, 17, 79–80
Christensen, P., 69
citations
  characteristics and writing of, 47–8, *47–8, 49–50*
  see also bibliographies
Clark, A., 69, 112
Climbie, Victoria legal case, 34–5
collaboration
  importance of parental role in early years learning, 37–8
collaboration, multi-agency

characteristics and impact of on
working patterns and trends, 35–7
exercise involving responses of, 85–90
exercise on use of concern-issue-conflict
involving, 84–5
need and importance for, 82–4
Commission for Equality and Human
Rights (CEHR), 71–2
Common Assessment Framework (CAF),
81–2
confidentiality
need in relation to practitioner
research, 71–3
Convention on the Rights of the Child
(United Nations), 66–7
cooperation, multi-agency *see*
partnerships, multi-agency
Cottrell, S., 117
cultures, child
importance of in current early years
learning environment, 94–7
play as consideration within early years
and learning environments, 98–9
*Curriculum Guidance for the Foundation
Stage* (2000), 31, 32–3, 35
CWDC (Children's Workforce
Development Council), 15, 17, 79–80

Dahlberg, G., 65, 70
David, T., 119
De Bono, E., 22
Desirable Learning Outcomes for
Children's Learning (SCAA) (1996),
30–31
Dewey, J., 52
Disability Discrimination Act (1995), 82
dispositions, child learning
salience in early years environments,
99–103, *101*
Dunlop, W. 97

Early Excellence Centre programme, 36
early years
definition, history and importance
educationally, 29–37
definition of work-based learning
within context of, 2–3
Early Years Foundation Stage (2007), 35,
67–8, 100
Early Years Professional Status (EYPS),
134–7

education *see* learners and learning
education, early years practitioner *see*
learners and learning, early-year
practitioner
Education Reform Act (1988), 30
Effective Provision of Pre-school
Education (EPPE) project, 15–16, 29–
30
Elfer, P., 111, 116
environments, early years learning
models of ethics within, 61–2, 63–4, *64*
role and salience of child culture and
play within, 94–9
salience and role of ethics within, 62–6,
62, 63, 64, 65, 66, 68–70
salience of autonomy within, 66–8
see also influences eg cultures, child;
dispositions, child learning
EPPE (Effective Provision of Pre-school
Education) project, 15–16, 29–30
Equality Act (2006), 71–2
Erikson, E., 54
ethics
need and role in relation to early years
learning environments and
research, 68–70, *68*
see also elements eg statements, ethical
ethics, early-year practitioner
need for in research, 68–70, *68*
salience in relation to early years and
learning environments, 62–6, *62,
63, 64, 65, 66*
see also elements eg integrity
Evans, L., 18
Every Child Matters: the Next Steps (2004),
35, 37, 68, 77, 85
evidence, research
nature, skills and methods of
collection,, 109–12, *113–15*
Excellence for all Children (1997), 103
Experience and Education (Dewey), 52
experiences, personal
early year student-practitioners, 124–30
EYPS (Early Years Professional Status),
134–7

Fabian, D., 97
FAIR model of ethics of early years
learning, 61–2, 63–4, *64*
Fleming, D., 96
frameworks, educational practice

multi-agency and partnership working, 82–4
on ethics of early years learning environments, 61–2, 63–4, *64*
see also models
see also name eg 'Grow Model'; Key Components Framework
Freud, S., 54
Frith, U., 63

Gardener, H., 55–6
'Grow Model' for work-based learning, 40–41, *41*

Hale, Z. (case study)
experiences as early years learning student, 128–30
Hatton, N., 4, 7
Haywood Metz, M., 5
Heron, J., 22
Honey, P., 51
Howes, C., 100–101, 101tab

Implementing the Disability Discrimination Act in Schools (2006), 82
integrity
need and role in relation to early years practitioner research, 71–3
interpretive research, 111

James, J., 100–101, 101tab

Katz, J., 70
Katz, L., 101
Kellet, M., 69
Key Components Framework (early years work-based learning), 22–7, *23–4, 26*
Kilderry, A., 17
kinaesthetic learners, 51
Kingston Friends Workshop Group (KFWG), 84

Laming report (2003), 34–5, 85
learners and learning
strengths and weaknesses of styles of, 50–53, *53*
theorists and their significance, *54–9*
see also skills, study
learners and learning, early-year practitioner
definition, history and importance educationally, 29–37

future research subjects, 119–20
nomenclature, 78–9, *79*
socio-educational context of work-based learning within, 2–3, 15–18
see also elements eg problems, solving of; questions and questioning; reflection, personal
  see also players eg parents; practitioners, early years learning; researchers and research, early years
legislation
need for early years practitioners to be knowledgeable about, 77–80, *79*
see also specific legislation eg Childcare Act; Children Act
Lewin, K., 111

McNiff, J., 105
Maslow, A., 22
methodology, early-years research
purpose and features, 105–9
see also elements eg evidence, research; observers and observation; reading
Miller, C., 84
Mills, C., 74
Mills, D., 74
models
child socialization, 100–101, *101*
ethics of early years learning environments, 61–2, 63–4, *64*
multi-agency and partnership working, 82–4
see also name eg 'Grow Model'; Key Components Framework
Montapert, A., 77
Moss, P., 65, 70
Mumford, A., 51

National Care Standards for Childcare Agencies (2003), 35
National Curriculum, 30, 98
National Foundation Stage Profile (2002), 33
National Literacy Strategy, 30, 31
National Numeracy Strategy, 30, 31
nomenclature
early years learning, 78–9, *79*
notes, taking of
characteristics, strengths and weaknesses, 43–6, *44, 45*

observers and observation, early-years
research
types, 116–17

Page, R., 5
parents
importance and collaborative role
within early years learning, 37–8
partnerships, multi-agency
exercise involving responses of, 85–90
exercise on use of concern-issue-conflict
involving, 84–5
need and importance for, 82–4
need for practitioners to be
knowledgeable and experienced,
77–80, 79
philosophies, early-year practitioner
salience in relation to early years and
learning environments, 62–6, 62,
63, 64, 65, 66
Piaget, J., 21–2, 29–30, 55, 63
Picasso, P., 93
plagiarism, 48
planning, research
timeline of, 117–19
play
role of as consideration in early years
learning environments, 98–9
policies, governmental
need for practitioners to be
knowledgeable about, 77–80, 79
see also specific policies eg Common
Assessment Framework; SureStart
initiatives
practical learners, 51
practice, reflective see reflection, personal
practitioners, early-years learning
case studies of as students, 124–
30
characteristics and impact of
collaboration patterns and trends
upon, 35–7
development of education for, 21–2
salience of philosophies, values
and beliefs in relation to
learning environments, 62–6,
62, 63, 64, 65, 66
see also influences impacting on eg
agencies, multiple; parents;
policies, governmental
see also practices eg learners and

learning, early-years
practitioner; researchers and
research, early-years
Primary National Strategy (2007), 97
problems, solving of
salience as element of early years
practitioner learning, 19–21, 21
Proust, M., 123

questions and questioning
categories of research, 107–9
salience as element of early years
practitioner learning, 19–21, 21

Rawlinson, G., 22
reading
characteristics, strengths and
weaknesses, 46
references and referencing
characteristics and writing of, 47–8, 47–
8, 49–50
see also bibliographies
reflection, personal
characteristics and importance, 52–3,
53
definition, characteristics and
limitations, 4
essentiality in practitioner research, 105
salience as element of early years
practitioner learning, 19–21, 21
Reggio Emilia approach to learning, 94,
111
researchers and research, early years
examples of future research subjects,
119–20
need for and role of ethical principles,
68–70, 68
need for and role of integrity of
practice, 71–3
purpose and validity, 4–5
see also methodology, early-years
research
see also elements eg questions and
questioning; reflection, personal
respect
salience in relation to children and
learning environments, 66–8
Rhedding-Jones, J., 19
Rideout, V., 96
Roberts-Holmes, G., 111
Robinson, C., 69

Rogers, A., 50
Rogers, C., 22
Rowson, R., 61–2, 63–4

Seagraves, L., 2
SEEC (South East England Consortium)
    for Credit Accumulation and
    Transfer, 2
Siraj-Blatchford, I., 73, 74
skills, research
    requirements for according to evidence,
        112, *113–15*
skills, study
    facets and characteristics of, 41–50, *42,*
        44, 45, 47, 48, 49–50
Skinner, B., 54
Smilansky, S., 55–6
Smith, A., 69–70
Smith, C., 71
Smith, D., 4, 7
socialization, child
    models of, 100–101, *101*
South East England Consortium for Credit
    Accumulation and Transfer (SEEC), 2
Special Educational Needs and Disability Act
    (2001), 82
statements, ethical, 112, 138–9
Stephen, C., 99
Stevenson, R.L., 105
Strategy for Childcare (2004), 79
students, early years learning
    case studies of experiences, 124–30
subjects, research
    examples of future possibilities, 119–20
    identification of, 107
SureStart initiative, 36, 80

Sylva, K., 55–6, 74

Tavistock method of observation, 116
teachers, early-years learning *see*
    practitioners, early-years learning
thinking, reflective *see* reflection, personal
timetables, research
    planning and example of, 117–19
Tomasello, M., 63

United Nations Convention on the Rights
    of the Child, 66–7

validity, research evidence, 112
values, early-year practitioner
    salience in relation to early years and
        learning environments, 62–6, *62,*
        63, 64, 65, 66
van Ijzendoorn, M., 95
Vermeer, H., 95
Victoria Climbie legal case, 34–5
Vygotsky, L., 29–30, 57–8

Walker D. (case study)
    experiences as early years learning
        student, 124–5
Walsh, D., 10
Whitehead, J., 105
workplaces
    practitioner learning within *see* learners
        and learning, early-years
        practitioner

years, early childhood *see* early years
Yelland, N., 17

EARLY YEARS FOUNDATIONS
Meeting the Challenge

Janet Moyles

With so many challenges facing early years professionals, there are continual dilemmas arising between doing what one knows is essentially 'right' for birth-to-five-year-olds from all backgrounds and conforming to the demands made by government and policy makers. This exciting and original book supports practitioners in thinking through their roles to meet some of the many issues they encounter.

Using the new *Early Years Foundation Stage* principles as its framework, the contributors support early years professionals in dealing with issues and challenges in a sensitive and professional manner, with particular emphasis upon the need for practitioners to personalise the requirements for each child in their care and to reflect closely upon their own and children's experiences.

The writers are all experienced and avid early years advocates. Their topics include: the changing landscape of early childhood, culture, identity and diversity, supporting playful learning, outdoor learning, documenting children's experiences, developing independence in learning, the meaning of being creative, play and mark-making in maths, and literacy.

Each section is introduced with some background research and information to provide evidence and guidance upon which practitioners can make their own decisions. Individual chapters include questions for reflection, points for discussion and suggestions for additional reading.

Early Years Foundations: Meeting the Challenge is essential reading for the full range of practitioners working and playing with birth-to-five-year-olds.

Contributors: *Deborah Albon, Pat Broadhead, Liz Brooker, Naima Browne, Elizabeth Carruthers, Tricia David, Dan Davies, Jackie Eyles, Hilary Fabian, Rose Griffiths, Alan Howe, Paulette Luff, Rod Parker-Rees, Theodora Papatheodorou, Emmie Short, David Whitebread, Marian Whitehead and Maulfry Worthington.*

Contents: *Notes on contributors – Introduction – Changing the landscape of early childhood – Section one: A unique child – Introduction – Primary communication: What can adults learn from babies? – Difference, culture and diversity: Challenges, responsibilities and opportunities – Identity and children as learners – Section two: Positive relationships – Introduction – Working together to support playful learning and transition – Somebody else's business: A parent's view of childhood – Coping with bereavement – Vision, mission, method: Challenges and issues in developing the role of the early years mentor teacher – Birth-to-three: The need for a loving and educated workforce – Section three: Enabling Environments – Introduction – The challenges of starting school – Children's outdoor experiences: A sense of adventure? – Written observations or walks in the park? Documenting children's experience – Food for thought: The importance of food and eating in early childhood practice – Section four: Learning and development – Introduction – Developing independence in learning – What does it mean to be creative? – Multi-modality, play and children's mark-making in maths – 'Hi Granny! I'm writing a novel.' Literacy in early childhood: Joys, issues and challenges – Endpiece – Appendix – Index.*

2007 308pp
978-0-335-22349-7 (Paperback) 978-0-335-22348-0 (Hardback)

DOING ACTION RESEARCH IN EARLY CHILDHOOD STUDIES

A Step-by-step Guide

Glenda Mac Naughton and Patrick Hughes

- Are you worried about doing your early years action research project?
- Does the thought of choosing the right research question feel daunting?
- Are you concerned about the challenges you might face?

If you answer 'yes' to any of these questions, then this is the book for you!

Written in a lively and accessible style, this is the essential step-by-step guide to conducting your own action research project. The book introduces and evaluates different approaches to action research and explores how they can be applied in early childhood settings to create positive change and to improve practice.

Using varied illustrations and case studies of contemporary projects in diverse early childhood contexts, the book addresses specific issues and challenges that you might face when conducting action research in such settings.

Each chapter offers gentle guidance and support at a specific stage of the research process, from choosing your initial topic to formulating your research question, through to sharing the lessons of your project.

The book's key features include:

- 16 'Steps' that walk you through the process of conducting your action research project
- References to real life research projects to illustrate key ideas, themes, practices and debates
- Advice on creating an action research journal, with sample extracts
- 'Thinking Boxes' in each chapter to encourage you to review and reflect on the chapter's contents as you plan your research project
- Checklists in each chapter of key concepts, processes and themes, together with further resources

The authors explore some difficult issues associated with action research, including ethics, rigour, validity, critical reflection, and social and professional change. They show that there is more than one 'right' way to perform an action research project and advise you how to choose an approach that is appropriate for your particular interests and circumstances.

Doing Action Research in Early Childhood Studies is an essential resource for students and practitioners of early childhood studies.

Contents: *Phase one: Choosing to change – Step 1 Choose a social practice to change or improve – Step 2 Ask a question about your chosen social practice – Phase two: Planning for a change – Step 3 Learn more about the action research family – Step 4 Learn more about your topic from the literature – Step 5 Learn more about your ethical responsibilities – Step 6 Learn about reflection, critical reflection and practice – Step 7 Map the practicalities of researching in your context – Step 8 Plan to make your research rigorous and valid – Phase three: Creating change – Step 9 Form an action research group – Step 10 Gather 'base line data – Step 11 Create a change and collect data about its effects – Step 12 Analyse your data – Step 13 Deepen and broaden your data and understandings – Step 14 Choose a social practice to change or improve, perhaps guided by a new research question – Phase four: Sharing the lessons – Step 15 Draw conclusions from your analysis – Step 16 Share the lessons of your project – References – Index.*

2008 208pp
978-0-335-22862-1 (Paperback) 978-0-335-22861-4 (Hardback)

DEVELOPING REFLECTIVE PRACTICE IN THE EARLY YEARS

Alice Paige-Smith and Anna Craft (eds)

Reflective practice is a vital aspect of working with young children and enables a deeper understanding of their learning and development. Whilst there is a long tradition among early childhood practitioners of closely observing children's learning so as to nurture and stimulate their development, they are increasingly expected to reflect on their own practice in a variety of ways, in order to enhance their professional development and improve their practice.

This book supports early years practitioners in articulating and understanding their own practice in greater depth, exploring some ways in which they can be encouraged to engage in reflecting on their practice. The book will help early years practitioners develop their reflective skills, enabling them to confidently articulate their practice, values and beliefs.

It offers opportunities to reflect on how theory, research and policy relate to distinct understandings of children's development and learning. By exploring different ways of understanding their own practice and linking this with theory and policy, practitioners are enabled to think about ways of improving their practice.

Developing Reflective Practice in the Early Years is essential reading for all early years practitioners working in early years settings for children aged 0-8 years, including nurseries, children's centres and schools.

Contributors: *Naima Browne, Anna Craft, Michael Craft, Caroline Jones, Alice Paige-Smith, Linda Pound, Michael Reed, Jonathan Rix, Elizabeth Wood.*

Contents: *List of figures – Notes on the contributors – Foreword – Acknowledgements – Introduction – Part 1: What does being a reflective early years practitioner involve? – Introduction to Part 1 – What does it mean to reflect on our practice? – Developing reflective practice – Exploring leadership: The roles and responsibilities of the early years professional – Part 2: How does reflective practice inform work with children? – Introduction to Part 2 – Children's social and emotional development – Inclusion and early years settings: What's your attitude? – Creativity and early years settings – Listening to young children: Multiple voices, meanings and understandings – Part 3: Leading edge practice: A community of reflective professionals – Introduction to Part 3 – Multi-agency working: Rhetoric or reality? – Reflective family-centred practices: Parents' perspectives and early intervention – Professional development through reflective practice – Reflection and developing a community of practice – Postscript: Democratic reflective practice in the early years.*

2007 216pp
978-0-335-22277-3 (Paperback) 978-0-335-22278-0 (Hardback)